WORKSHOP PROJECTS

BY
DYSON WATKINS

British Library Cataloguing-in-Publication-Data: a catalogue record of this book is held by the British Library.

First Printing 2008

ISBN No. 978-0-9547131-8-8

Published in Great Britain by:

CAMDEN MINIATURE STEAM SERVICES
Barrow Farm, Rode, Frome, Somerset. BA11 6PS
www.camdenmin.co.uk

Camden stock one of the widest selections of engineering, technical and transportation books to be found; contact them at the above address for a copy of their latest free Booklist, or see their website.

Layout and design by Camden Studios.

Printed by the MPG Books Group in the UK

CONTENTS:

INTRODUCTION

My aim in writing this book, as its name suggests, is to provide a source of projects that can be made by the craftsman who possesses machining facilities, most of which can be carried out with a lathe and a drilling machine. Milling, where required, can be carried out on the lathe using a vertical slide. In the event that the book is used by a newcomer to engineering, be it model engineering, or tool making as a support for another hobby, I have included projects of a varying order of difficulty. Early chapters will also be provided with a list of the process operations involved in the making. The tools presented will provide a degree of progression, particularly valuable should the material be used as an educational resource. A star rating has been adopted to provide an indication of the degree of difficulty. Elements of bench work have been included as well as machining. The intention is to provide help for the beginner through the making of these tools and thereby avoid some of the pitfalls that could deter progress where more demanding processes are encountered. The amount of help with processes will be reduced with progression through the book, as this will become less necessary. It is hoped that the projects will provide a source of enjoyment in their making also, and if this involves learning something new during progress through the book, then my aim will be doubly satisfied.

Enjoy.   Dyson Watkins November 2008

DIE HOLDERS

PROCESSES

■ **Turning and facing**
■ **Centre drilling**
■ **Boring to diameter and to depth**
■ **Parting off**
■ **Drilling and tapping**
■ **Taper turning using the compound slide**
■ **Silver soldering**

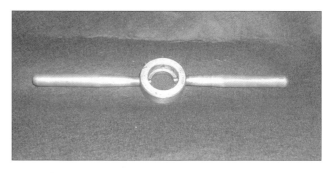

Photo 1.1: Completed Die Holder

The first project is a set of die holders. Make the sizes that match the dies you have available at present. Should you decide to make more than one size, then machine two together which will save both time and material. Cut the blank long enough to allow cleaning up both end faces and to allow parting off after the turning and boring operations have been completed. Sizes are provided in tabulated form so that dimensions for any particular holder can be read off without repetition of the drawing.

All turning can be carried out in the three-jaw chuck because a high degree of concentricity is not too important. Grip the blank so that enough projects to allow the outside diameter to be cleaned up. Face the end and follow this by centre drilling the end. Do not be tempted to drill into the end face without centre drilling first as the drill will attempt to skate over the face with the possibility of breakage. Use drills progressively greater in size and finish off by boring if necessary. Boring will become more desirable when larger diameters are required.

Bore out the die recess, using a die to try the fit as the final size is approached. The depth of the recess needs to be accurate so that the grub screws line up with the

Table 1.2   Die Holder Dimensions

DIE O/D	ØA	ØB	ØC	ØD	E	E/2	F	F/2	M
13/16	0.817	1.125	0.625	0.187	0.375	0.187	0.25	0.125	M3
1	1.005	1.5	0.75	0.25	0.450	0.225	0.375	0.1875	M4
1 5/16	1.317	1.75	1.0	0.3125	0.562	0.281	0.440	0.220	M4
1 ½	1.505	2.0	1.25	0.375	0.625	0.312	0.50	0.25	M5
2	2.005	2.625	1.375	0.375	0.75	0.375	0.625	.312	M5

Table 1.3 Handle Dimensions - see drawing No. 1.4

DIE O/D	øD	øJ	L	N
3/16	0.187	0.375	3.0	0.2
1	0.25	0.375	3.5	0.18
1 5/16	.3125	0.5	4.0	0.20
1 1/2	0.375	0.5	4.5	0.25
2	0.375	0.5	5.5	0.312

dimples in the edges of the die. Reverse in the chuck and machine the other end. Most of the marking out can be carried out while the work is still in the lathe. Apply some marking blue, or permanent felt-tip marker, which I tend to use nowadays. Set a scribing block to the lathe centre height, and scribe a line across the end face and along each side. Next set the line just made by turning the chuck by hand and setting it vertical using a square. Scribe another horizontal line as before. You now need another two lines one on either side of the last one, spaced at 45°. A protractor can be used for setting these two angles. Reverse the work in the chuck and do the same for the other end (if making two holders). The remainder of the marking out can be completed with the work-piece set on a surface table, or a piece of plate glass. The marked hole centres can now be centre punched lightly. When drilling the holes, make sure that each one is radially accurate. Tap the holes for the grub screws. The holes for the handles need to be counter bored just far enough to provide a flat surface. This might appear to be unnecessary, but the recess thus provided will allow

the silver solder to flow between the parts of the joint without spilling over and causing unsightly blobs.

The handles are straightforward and should not require much explanation. The work is set in the chuck with about ½in. protruding. Turn the little spigot first on all handles. Set up the top slide to 3° and turn all the tapers. Grinding up a form tool can do the rounded ends, otherwise rough turn the ends free hand and finish up with a file and emery cloth. The handles are not knurled. Knurling looks attractive but can cause blisters where a large amount of screw cutting is carried out.

Silver soldering is carried out next. A suitable solder diameter would be ⅟32in. made into a ring by winding it round a drill shank to form a coil, and then snipping off one at a time. Use a drill shank somewhat smaller in diameter than the ring size to allow for spring in the wire. The work is set up vertically with the lower handle held in a vice. *Easy-flo* Silver solder with *Easy-flo* flux will give excellent results. Clean the joint surfaces prior to heating the work and mix a little clean water with the flux powder to form a cream consistency then stir in a tiny drop of washing up liquid to improve the wetting quality. Try to bring both parts up to temperature together, as the solder will tend to flow over the hottest surface first, and don't overheat. Stop heating when a fillet is seen to form. Do not quench in cold water before the work has had time to cool naturally as doing so will weaken the joint considerably. Any excess flux can be removed later by immersing in hot water and then drying thoroughly. A good clean up with fine emery cloth followed by light oiling will complete the work.

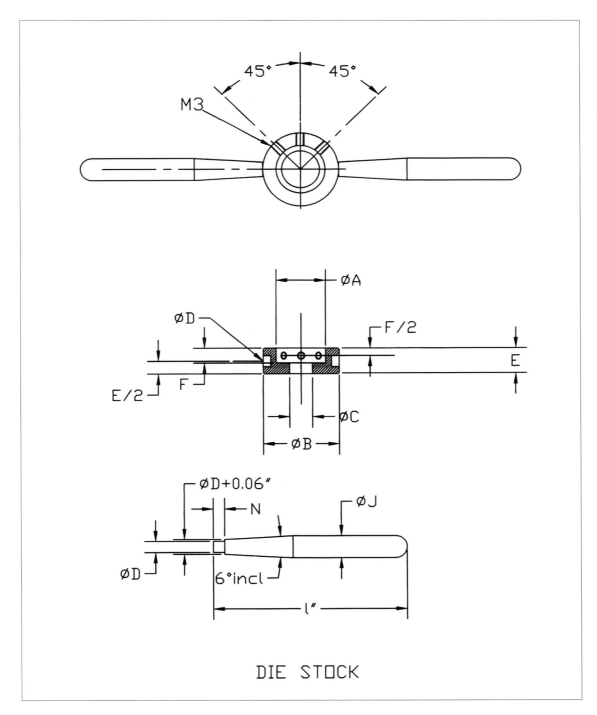

DIE STOCK

Drawing 1.4: Die Holder

MACHINE CLAMP

....

PROCESSES

- ☐ **Marking out**
- ☐ **Sawing**
- ☐ **Filing**
- ☐ **Turning**
- ☐ **Milling (or filing)**

Photo 1.5:
Machine clamp in use on drilling machine

This piece of equipment is well worth the effort of making, and is a desirable piece of kit, being an exercise in bench fitting and machining, with some items requiring turning. The scale can be modified to suit the size of machine on which it is to be used. I tend to use it mainly on the drilling machine (Photo 1.5), which has provision for a 10mm Tee nut. The

clamp is a Godsend when drilling small and awkward pieces which are difficult to grip in the vice perhaps through not possessing parallel faces, and particularly when drilling sheet materials which have a nasty habit of pulling themselves up the drill and whirling round like a proverbial scythe! The gadget is not intended to drive the common slotted bar clamps and Tee bolt assemblies into instant obsolescence, but to complement that which is already commonplace in the workshop. It will be found useful due to the speed with which it can be set up without need for a spanner, or having to hunt for bits of packing. It does provide something pleasurable to make from scraps straight out of the junk bin. The size can be changed to suit if required, by scaling down.

I do not claim that the tool is entirely original, because I have seen something similar in the past, which was devised as a test piece for apprentices. I have however chosen a construction method whereby it may be dismantled if necessary, perhaps for internal cleaning. It is very robust and should last a lifetime.

SIDES

Photo 1.6: Sides shown have been cut from ¼in. steel

These are made from mild steel plate, the thickness I had available being ¼in., although thinner plate could be used with corresponding minor changes in some of the mating components. Mark out one side completely, and centre punch the hole positions. Saw the profile leaving a little for final filing and finishing to size. Drill the holes to size after clamping it onto a second piece that will form the second side, thus ensuring accurate alignment of the holes. Then scribe the profile on to the second piece using the finished side as a template. This will make certain that the two sides should end up the same size. The two parts can then be bolted together and finished as one. Draw file the edges, and emery cloth to a fine finish. Rub on a light coating of oil to help keep rust at bay until later.

SPACERS

These are turned from mild steel rod to finish at ½in. diameter, and 0.630in./0.635in. in length so as to provide a little clearance for the moving parts. The

Photo 1.7: Detail view of spacers

spacers are drilled through 4.2mm diameter and tapped M5 through from one end. This will avoid having a pitch mismatch somewhere in the middle. Start off the tap by holding it in the tail stock, and rotating the headstock chuck by hand. When the tap has made a good start, the thread can be completed by using a tap wrench. It is important to make the spacers all the same length within the tolerance, which imparts a good fit to the moving internal components. An adjustable back stop will be found very useful for this operation, as when the length of the first component has been set, the remainder are simply turned off to the same length against the stop.

It is worth carrying out a quick trial assembly (Photo 1.8) at this stage to check that all is well.

SWINGING ARM SIDE PLATES

For this item we require 8in. of bright mild steel strip ¾in. x 3⁄16in. thick. As in the case of the side plates, mark out one side, and after completing it, clamp it to the other side, and drill through both pieces in the three hole positions. Bolt the pieces together with close fitting bolts and finish the second piece using the first as a template.

SWINGING ARM SPACERS

Photo 1.8: A trial assembly is a useful check

Photo 1.9: Machining a flat on the link

Make the spacers from a high carbon, or tool steel, as these parts will be subjected to stress and wear. Alternatively, case harden them. Make sure when these are turned that the projecting lugs are concentric. Note that the lengths of the lugs are turned to suit the thickness of the material used for the side plates.

LINK

This component requires setting up in the four-jaw chuck. Square off one end and remove from the lathe to mark the position of the centre. Punch the position lightly and accurately, so that a centre finder can be used to set it up accurately in the four-jaw chuck. Drill and ream the ⁵⁄₁₆in. diameter hole. Next mark out the remainder and either drill the other two holes carefully in the bench drill using parallel packing for squareness, or set up the vertical slide and do the job in style! If you decide on using the slide then the two flats can be machined instead of sawing and filing. It's good to have a choice.

CLAMP SCREW AND TOMMY BAR

These are made from mild steel. A length of 4½in. x ⅝in. diameter will be needed. Hold it in the three-jaw chuck, face and centre one end lightly. Re-chuck with 4in. protruding, and support the end on the tail stock centre. Turn the diameter down to 10mm for a length of 3¼in.. Turn the undercut at the head end down to the depth of thread. Set up the change wheels for a pitch of 1.5mm, and with the appropriate screw cutting tool in the toolpost, proceed to cut the thread.

Remove any roughness from the crests with a fine file and finish with a touch of emery cloth, or use a 1.5mm chaser, or run a M10 die down! Next turn down the small end to ⁵⁄₁₆in. to give a running fit in the link not forgetting the chamfer at the end and the groove for the retaining screw. It would be a good idea to check the relative position of the hole in the link and that of the groove before machining the groove so that the end of the screw is able to bottom in the ⁵⁄₁₆in. hole. This will avoid the possibility of the retaining pin having to carry any shear load during normal clamp operation. Next, reverse in the chuck without tightening too much, thereby damaging the threads, and finish the turning on the head end. Lastly, set up in the vertical slide, or otherwise, and drill the tommy bar hole. Remove any burrs and polish up in the lathe. (Should there be any anxiety at the prospect of screw cutting the clamp screw, it can be made from two pieces, and screw cutting can be avoided for the present by utilising a length of M10 studding). Lastly set up in the vertical slide, or otherwise, and drill the tommy bar hole. Remove any burrs and polish up in the lathe.

Photo 1.10: Detail shot of tommy bar and screw

The tommy bar is made from ⁵⁄₁₆in. diameter mild steel rod, with ends turned from ½in. diameter bar. The ends are turned ½in. long with .06in. chamfers each end. The holes are drilled to ¼in. diameter, and the rod is turned down to this size for a length of ⁹⁄₁₆in. to allow enough material to form the rivetted ends. A 0.05in. chamfer is enough to provide a secure rivetted end on each boss. Peen over one end so as to fill the chamfer, and face off flush. Do remember to pass the tommy bar through the end hole in the screw before peening the second end. The second end can be faced off in the lathe with care, allowing the screw to hang down in front of the chuck. As long as the tommy bar is a loose running fit in the screw head, there should be no tendency for it to rotate with the machine. Go carefully with this operation, and keep fingers out of the way!

SWIVEL NUTS

These are made from ¾in. diameter mild steel bar. Mount in the three-jaw chuck, allowing about 1in. to protrude. Just clean up the outside diameter lightly so as to true up, and machine the end spigot to give a nice fit in its mating hole in one of the side plates. Reverse in a four-jaw chuck and clock up true using a dial indicator. Machine the remaining spigot and check its fit.

Next set it up in the vertical slide, and centre-drill/drill a 8.5mm diameter hole through, taking out the parallel packing from underneath before you do so! Then start off an M10 tap in the hole, holding it initially in the three-jaw chuck. Finish off using a tap wrench. In the event that a vertical slide is not available, all is not lost! The flat can be put on with a file. The purpose of the flat is to allow a greater degree of travel for the swinging arm.

DRAW BOLT

This can be made up from a length of M10 studding. The disk at the lower end is tapped M10 and is screwed on to the studding to leave 3 to 4mm proud. The end is carefully peened over to fill the countersink in the disk, and then faced off flush. The top end of the studding can be slotted if desired, so that it can be adjusted from above using a screwdriver, although not really necessary, as in most cases access is easy from beneath the table. The exception is in the case of a milling machine, where the clamp is equally useful.

ASSEMBLY

The various components are shown in position in photo 1.11.

FINISH

If the facilities exist, then I would suggest oil blacking, or chemical blacking which is reasonably hard wearing, and can withstand scratching from whirling swarf. Finally I would add that there is only one thing better than making one of these clamps, and that is to make a pair.

**Photo 1.11:
Components for the machine clamp**

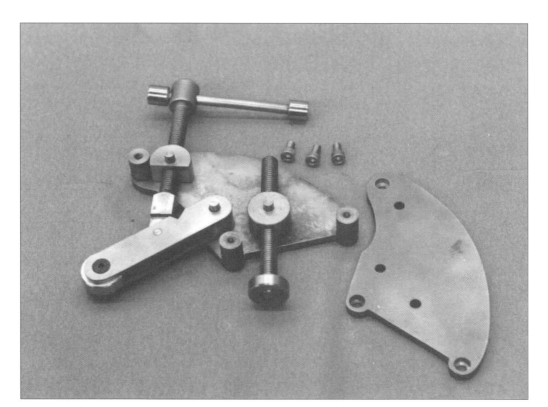

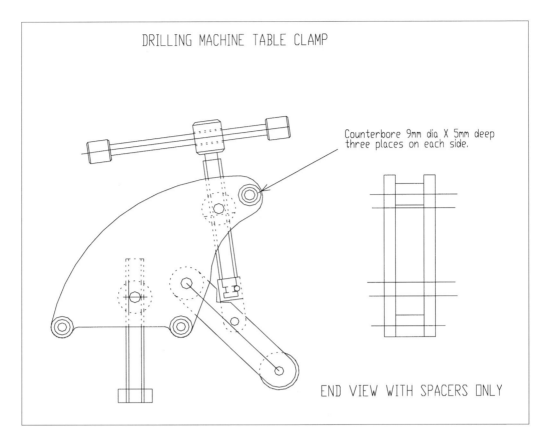

Drawing 1.12

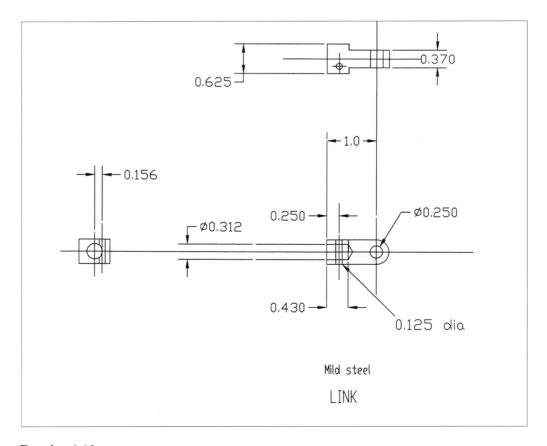

Drawing 1.13

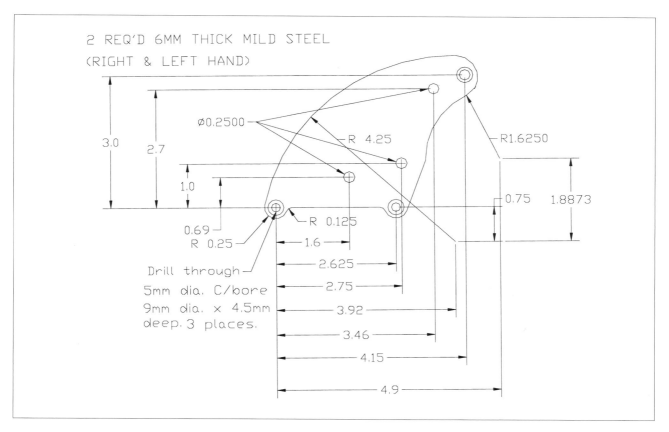

Drawing 1.14: Side plate

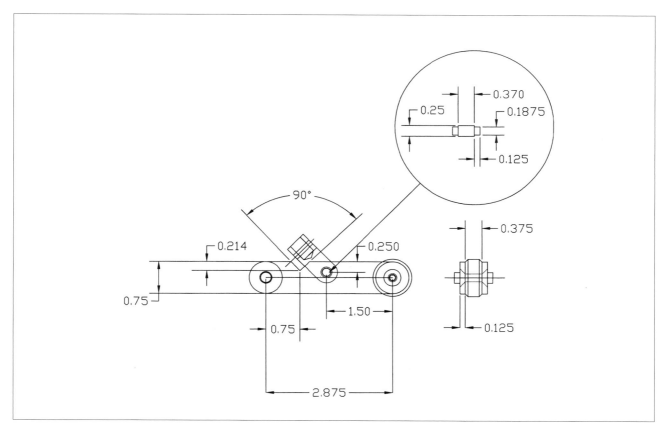

Drawing 1.15: Swinging arm sub-assembly

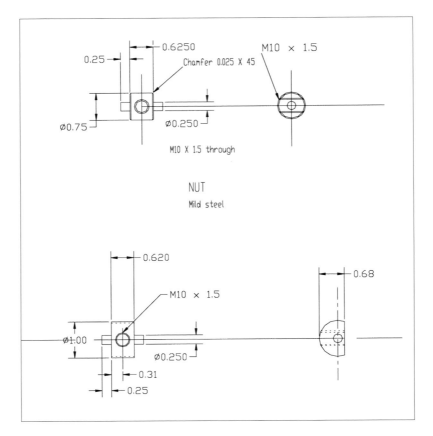

Drawing 1.16

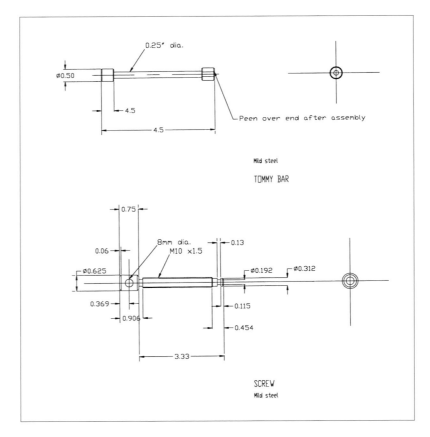

Drawing 1.17

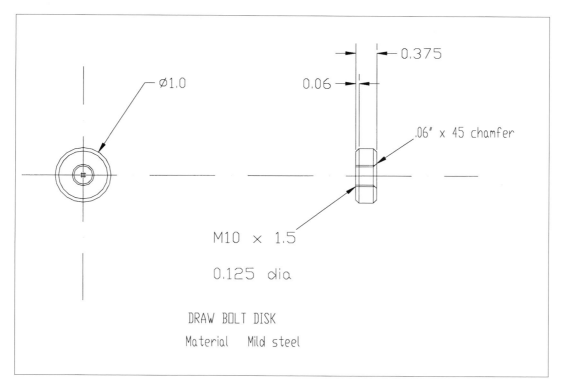

Drawing 1.18

CROSS DRILLING JIG FOR THE LATHE

PROCESSES

- **Turning and facing**
- **Taper turning**
- **Drilling**
- **Boring**
- **Milling**
- **Bench work**

There have been many instances in the past when the need to drill a hole through the cross section of a circular rod or bar has cropped up. A few examples which come to mind are holes for split pins, holes for the handles of 'T' wrenches, lathe chuck key handles. The list goes on and on. In the absence of a milling machine where the position of the bar centre can be accurately found, the method could possibly be a trifle hit or miss. The photograph (2.1) shows the jig in use for cross drilling and reaming the shaft for the milling attachment described later in this book. This little tool removes all the uncertainty previously encountered in this operation, and avoids the necessity for setting up the vertical slide.

The jig is very easy to use, the part to be drilled is placed in the 'vee' location groove, the position of the

Photo 2.1:
Cross drilling jig in use

hole to be drilled is adjusted in line with the lathe axis, the swing clamp is brought into position and tightened up. This procedure can be done on the bench, or with the jig secured in the tailstock, either way offers no difficulty. The hole is then started with a centre drill, and completed with a drill of the required diameter. The drilled hole will be accurately placed (providing of course that the tailstock has been correctly set on centre!)

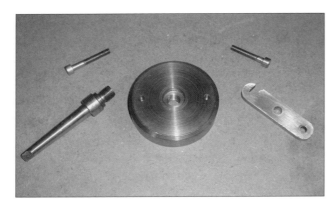

Photo 2.2: Component parts of the jig

TAPER SHANK

The first component to be made is the shank, and here you have to choose the size that suits you best. My lathe was an ancient Drummond 'M', which had a No. 1 Morse taper, but should you require a different size,

then the appropriate dimensions are easily obtained. Alternatively, you can make yours as drawn, and simply use a Morse taper adapter sleeve. The choice is yours. Material for any part can be changed, as I would expect most constructors to use whatever they happened to have available. Generally, mild steel will be fine and the 'Vee' location pad would benefit from being case hardened to resist wear, or made from silver steel and hardened. Take a length of bar and hold it in the three-jaw chuck. Face and centre one end. Re-chuck so that enough of the bar protrudes from the chuck to machine the taper, supporting the end with the tailstock centre. Here you can use your own favourite method for producing the taper, but in the event that any constructor is uncertain of this procedure, then I will describe the method I use. I do not claim that it is the only way, or that it is the best, but only that it works for me.

Firstly, skim the bar and check by measurement that the machine is set up to turn parallel. If it is, then place a dial indicator in the toolpost and swivel the top slide over to the approximate half angle of the taper to be machined. Knowing the taper per inch required, advance the top slide one inch and observe the reading on the gauge, adjusting carefully until the reading corresponds to half the taper per inch for one inch of travel of the slide. For most modellers' machines the tapers will be either No. 1 or No. 2, with a smaller

Drawing 2.3: Morse Taper Arbor No. 1 MT

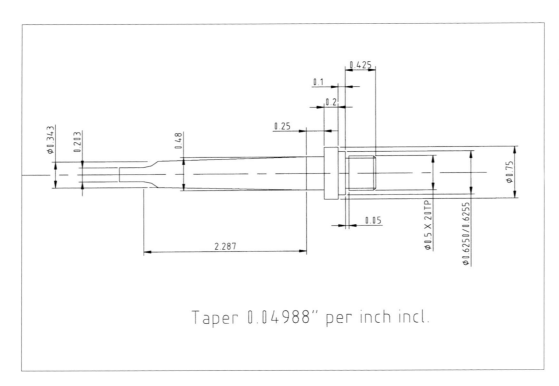

Taper 0.04988" per inch incl.

number of No. 3 M.T. The taper per inch for these tapers is very close to 0.05in., and should a dial indicator be unavailable, then alternatively, advance the cutting tool from a point where it just leaves contact with the work a distance of one inch, at which point it should be just possible to slide a .025in. feeler gauge in between the tool and the work. Having set up the angle, machine away the waste until the taper is about three quarters of the final length. It is possible at this stage to try on a sleeve to check the angle, because the tang end will not reach its slot. Next without removing the work from the chuck, try on an appropriate M.T. sleeve having very lightly smeared the inside of the sleeve with highspot marking blue. Note how far the part projects from the mouth of the tailstock. Assuming that the taper is correct and that the marking blue is transferred all along the shank, the amount which remains to be removed can be easily calculated. Simply multiply the excess length by 0.025 to give the depth of cut remaining. For example, let us assume that the tang projects too far out of the tailstock barrel by 0.75in.. then , 0.75 X 0.025 = 0.0187in. which is the depth of the final cut required to allow the shank to enter the barrel to its correct depth.

The next job is to file (or mill) the sides of the tangs. Make certain to end up with a tang which is in the middle of the shank, and not offset to one side. Check the fit with an appropriate sleeve. Next remove the chuck from the headstock and clean out the taper thoroughly. Locate the newly completed taper shank into the headstock spindle; tap it gently to make sure that it will not become loose during the subsequent machining operations.

Turn the 0.75in. diameter first, followed by the 0.6255/0.6250in. register diameter. Turn the undercut to a few 'thou' smaller in diameter than the root diameter of the thread to be cut. I decided to produce a 20 T.P.I. thread which corresponds to ½in. U.N.F. The root diameter of this is 0.4387in. from tables, but 0.438in. will be fine. Do remember that if you wish to cut the unified form that the included angle is 60 deg., not 55 deg. as for Whitworth. I made my choice because I happened to have a ½in. U.N.F. tap with which I could clean out the internal thread later on. Set up the screwcutting tool squarely to ensure that the flank angles will be symmetrical, and having set up the machine for screwcutting, proceed to cut the thread. A useful object to have at hand is a matching nut with which to test the fit as the work approaches the finished size. A thread chaser is also handy to clean up the thread during finishing. Finish the shank by facing off to length, and drilling a shallow hole in the end, say, ⁵⁄₁₆in. in diameter to serve as a clearance hole when the jig is in use.

Drawing 2.4: Assembly drawing with a component shown ready for drilling

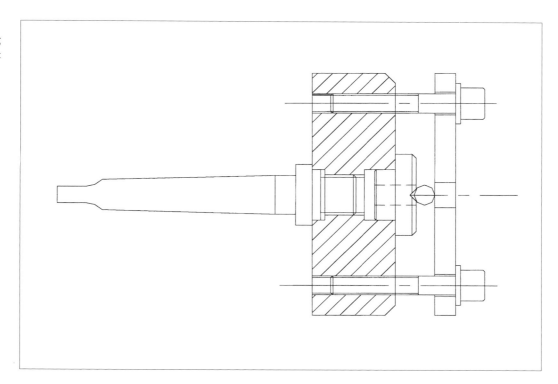

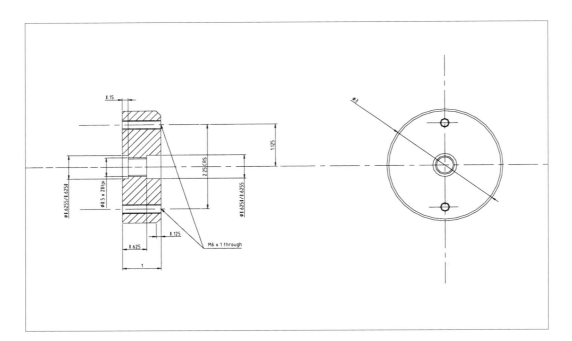

Set up the blank as accurately as possible using a dial indicator in a four-jaw chuck. Face the blank and centre drill the end, following it with a 7/16in. diameter drill straight through to remove the bulk of the waste. Set up a boring tool and bore out the hole to the root diameter of the thread, which is 0.446in. for ½in. U.N.F. Change over to the internal screwcutting tool, and cut the internal thread, checking from time to time for fit.

Next, change back to the boring tool (which should be capable of producing a square end face in the bore) and bore out the register counterbore, and check for a good fit. Before reversing to work on the other end, a nice touch is to lightly chamfer the leading edge of the thread. I use the screwcutting tool for this.

Set up the blank for machining the other end face using the dial indicator as before for accuracy, but additionally using small parallels to set the machined face square up against the chuck face. I use a couple of H.S.S. tool bits for this. Most importantly, don't forget to take them out before starting the machine, you could end up toothless or worse when they fly out! Face the other end leaving a chamfer on the outer edge. Then bore out the recess for the 'V' pads. Put a small lead in chamfer in the mouth of the bore to make the loading of alternative 'V' pads an easy operation. Then chamfer the leading thread as before.

Replace the chuck with the finished taper shank, after thoroughly cleaning both the shank and the spindle

bore, and screw the body into place. Skim the outside diameter to clean up. It is a good idea at this point to clock up the front face of the body to check that all is square. If any error manifests itself, then the face can be lightly skimmed to make it run absolutely true. The same comment applies to the bore, and if this has to be bored out slightly to square up, then do it now, and increase the corresponding diameter on the 'V' pads when they are turned to provide a nice fit. The better alternative is to make the bore slightly undersize initially and finish to size at this stage.

Remove from the lathe after making a light witness mark in the form of a 2.25in. diameter circle, ready for drilling the holes for the M6 threads. The drill size is 5mm. Start the tap holding it in the drill chuck to ensure that the thread cut will be true, and once it has had a good start then remove from the chuck and finish the tapping right through. Finally chamfer both ends of the tapped holes.

SWING CLAMP

Little need be said regarding the making of this component as it is quite straightforward. The bolt holes are 7.0mm diameter. It is better not to make the centre hole too big otherwise the clamp will be weakened. If it is desired to drill larger holes, then a wider clamp can be substituted which will obviate the problem. If possible then the clamp would benefit from case hardening to protect from wear and tear.

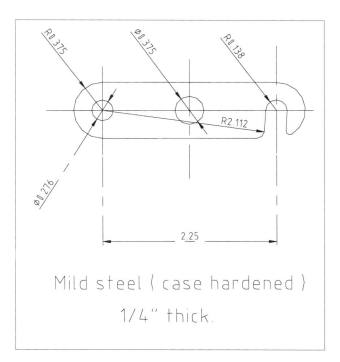

Drawing 2.6: Swing Clamp

"V" PADS

These need care in making in order to end up with a good degree of accuracy. First of all, turn the outside diameter followed by the diameter to fit the bore in the body. Part off slightly over length. It is worth turning a few of these so that "V" grooves of different sizes can be made to suit different diameters of bar. If you are fortunate enough to possess a milling maching, then the groove can be milled out.

If not, then lesser mortals, myself included, need to set up a vertical slide. The photograph depicts my lash up which is quite effective, traverse being in the vertical plane. Clocking up the vice jaw is not important this

Photo 2.7: Milling vee groove

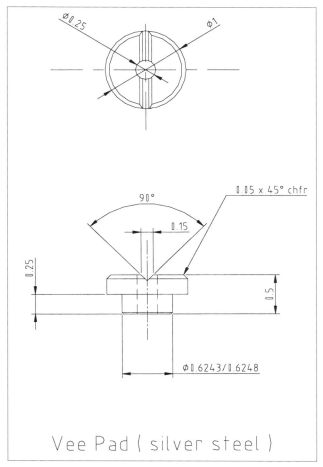

Drawing 2.8: Vee Pad

time, but it is important to make sure that the face of the pad is truly vertical clamping, directly on to the front of the slide if necessary. The dial indicator can be put to good use once again for this check. When the pad is correctly set up, take a light cut somewhere near the centre traversing the cut right across the face. Measure how far off centre the groove happens to be. If for example it is .025in. off centre, then the amount to move in order to correct the position (during each subsequent cut) can be calculated as follows.

DEPTH OF CORRECTING CUT
= 0.25in. X 1.414 = .035in.

A further refinement which could be added after making the tool, is to add an adjustable stop against which to set the work to be drilled. This would need to be removable in the event of requiring to drill a hole some way from the end of the work and could be added if necessary. The end stop would be useful in the event that a number of identical parts need to be cross drilled.

SWAN NECKED TURNING TOOL HOLDER

Photo 3.1: Swan necked tool holder mounted on toolpost

The swan necked turning tool has been with the engineering fraternity for many years, but nowadays does not appear to be in general use, which I believe to be a pity, since it can solve many a problem of poor 'finish' from 'chatter' marks. The toolholder to be described is most useful if only for the reason that it uses for its cutting tips discarded end mills or slot drills previously consigned to the workshop scrap bin. If you belong to the majority of machining enthusiasts who occasionally suffer from the 'chatter mark syndrome', then read on .

Drawing 3.2:
Tangential cutting force on a
conventional solid tool.

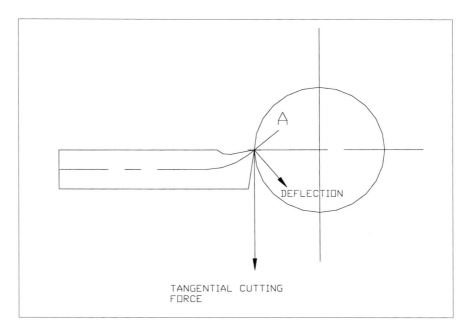

Numerous designs have appeared over the years, many of which favoured the forged type of body with a butt welded cutting tip. When the tip finally wore out and gave up the ghost, the tool ended up in the bin! This was one of the reasons for making a tool holder, as the tips would be replaceable. The other reason being that of versatility, as the tool can be furnished with a variety of tips suitable for turning generally as well as for screwcutting. Another point which is most useful is that since the tips are cylindrical, they can be adjusted slightly by rotating them in order to adjust clearance and rake angles.

The principle of operation of the swan necked tool is quite easy to understand if the geometry of the setup is considered.

A conventional solid tool (Fig. 3.2) under load will deflect in such a way that the cutting tip moves further into the material being cut, even though the amount may be very small. This has the effect of suddenly increasing the tool tip load disproportionately with the effect of removing a tiny extra deep bite out of the workpiece, and can set up vibration resulting in the too familiar chatter pattern. The swan necked tool (Fig. 3.3) on the other hand, has its centre of bending raised artificially, so that when it deflects under load, the tip tends to move away from the workpiece, thus reducing the load on the tip and the vibration pattern is thus avoided.

Construction of the tool is straightforward, being made from a piece of 12mm gauge plate. Not much need be said regarding its manufacture as this is an easy little project. It is however worth mentioning that the slot should be cut last of all, so that all the other machining operations can be carried out in 'solid' material. The slot width is not critical in the least, and can be cut using a slitting saw, or sawn out using a hacksaw. Mark out the profile of the tool on the metal, and either drill

Drawing 3.3:
Tangential cutting force on a
swan necked tool holder

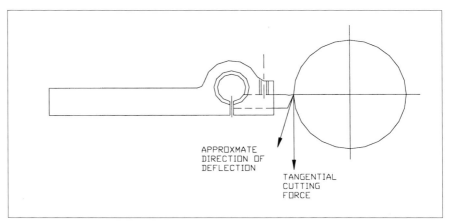

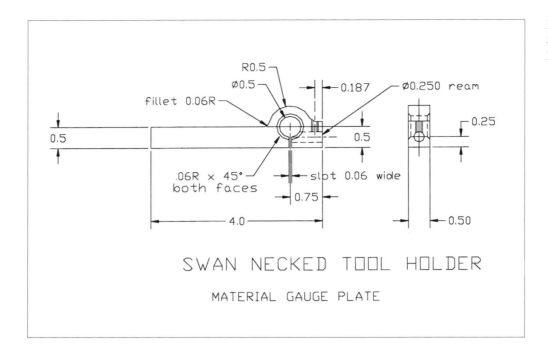

out the 12mm dia. hole on the drilling or milling machine, or clamp it on the faceplate of your lathe and machine it out. Whichever method you decide to use, it will be a little easier to carry out while the metal is relatively square and easily clamped. Chamfer the edges of the hole next. Remove the bulk of the waste from the shank and clean the radiussed section. Next drill and ream the hole for the tool bit. Choose whichever

diameter suits best according to your 'supply' of tool bits. The toolholder is also handy for use on the shaping machine if such a machine is available.

The tool holder can be made from mild steel should gauge plate be unavailable, but the clamping face will tend to be more susceptible to damage by the clamping screws.

TAILSTOCK DIE HOLDER

Photo 3.5:
Tailstock die holder
in use on lathe

If at any time you have been faced with the problem of cutting threads that have to be free from drunken thread syndrome, then this little project is a definite must for you. Most readers will very likely have come across this tool at sometime or another, but if you don't already possess one, then now is the time to start making it, and once made, you will wonder how on earth you ever managed without it.

DESCRIPTION

The tool is simply a sliding die holder supported on a taper shanked arbor held in the tailstock. Two heads are made which cater for four popular diameters of dies, namely 13/16in., 1in., 15/16in. and l½in. The die in use is held in the appropriate recess by three grub screws, which are carefully tightened so as to compress the die progressively so that the resulting thread ends up at the correct diameter. More about this later. The tailstock must of course be set on centre prior to this operation.

MAKING

The arbor is made from a length of ¾in. dia. bar. One end is faced and centred, then gripped near one end, and supported at the other by the tailstock centre. A light cut is then taken along the bar to true up its surface. Several methods are suitable for machining the taper, and the use of a dial indicator is probably the easiest, so this method will be described next.

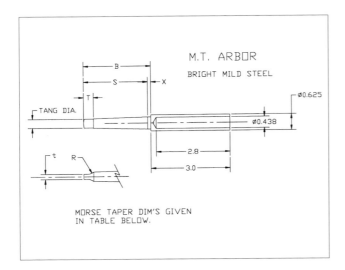

Drawing. 3.6: Morse taper arbor

Photo 3.7: Component parts of the die holder

The taper in terms of the change in radius per inch length needs to be calculated, or read from tables, such as Zeus, which most constructors seem to have in their possession. Set over the compound slide (or top slide) as accurately as possible to half the included angle of the taper. Set up the dial indicator in the tool holder, so that it rests on the skimmed part of the bar. If the compound slide is now advanced a distance of 1in. then if the angle is correctly set the dial indicator will move through a distance equal to the sine of half the included angle. To save anyone the bother of thumbing through tables or hunting for a calculator, the dial indicator travel corresponding to Morse taper Numbers 1, 2 and 3 are given in the table at the end of the article.

For those less fortunate constructors who do not have a dial indicator, the following method is also suitable. Set up the half angle as before, as accurately as possible. Next set up a cutting tool in the tool post and wind it in until it just makes contact with a 0.025in. feeler gauge which is held against the work piece. Withdraw the feeler gauge, and wind back the top slide until the tool just makes contact with the work. The distance traversed should be 1in. as in the previous method. It is worth mentioning that the sine of the half angle is almost the same as the tangent because the angle is so small, so if anyone wishes to check the dimensions using trigonometry, it will be evident that this fact is quite true for the degree of accuracy required.

Yet a third method, which is perhaps cheating just a little, is to set up a drill having the required size of taper shank between centres and set up the compound slide to the same taper, either with a dial indicator, or with feeler gauges. Choose whichever method suits best.

Having set the angle accurately, machine the taper according to the chosen size and then, after removing the chuck, mount the newly machined taper in the headstock taper after cleaning out the head stock taper thoroughly. Then machine the parallel portion of the arbor to 0.625in. diameter having first drilled the hole down the centre. The hole incidentally will be found to be very useful when making long screw threads, as they will have the space available to project into the hole.

DIE HOLDERS

It is immaterial as to which die holder is made next, as the methods used are the same for both sizes. If bright bar is used which is clean and undamaged, set it up in the four-jaw chuck to run true. It can with care be set up in the three-jaw chuck if the latter is reasonably accurate and the jaws in good condition. Face the end of the bar, and drill out the waste as far as possible so as to leave just a little for boring out the 0.625in. centre hole. If a 0.625in. reamer is available, then it would be worth reaming the hole, in which case the die holders should be made before the arbor, and then the corresponding dimension on the arbor could be machined to the desired degree of fit using the die holder as a gauge. Having bored out the centre hole to give a good sliding fit on the arbor, proceed to bore out the recess for the die. It is a good idea to use a die to test the fit, as the die should not have to be entered into the recess with any degree of force, which would of course have the tendency to close the die in use and

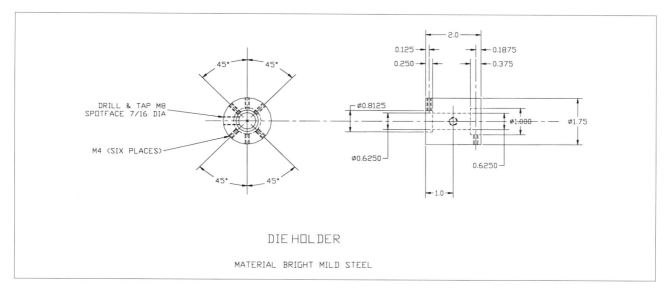

Drawing 3.8

make it cut an undersized thread. Next reverse in the chuck and bore out the other end to suit the corresponding die.

The tapped holes for securing the die need to be marked out next, and it is worth reflecting at this stage as to the most convenient point on the holder to place them. In use, the peg fitted into the side of the holder will generally be horizontal, projecting towards the turner and supported on a steady held in the tool post (at any rate, that's how I do it), so for ease of adjustment, it is most convenient to position the screws on the top, which means that for the holder on the other end, the screws will be in the opposite side! It does not matter however if they are on the same side, it only means that the holder has to be turned over for adjustment; no sweat. The tapped holes are 45 deg. apart, set in from the mouth of the recess by a distance equal to half the depth of the recess, which is also half the thickness of the die. The sizes of screws used are in no way critical as long as their points mate up with the recesses in the dies used. I used 4 B.A. on mine as these were available. Next drill and spot face the hole where the peg fits into the side. A suitable thread size would be ~⅛in. B.S.F. or M8 if preferred.

The two pegs are made to suit the lathe, being made longer if required to suit the space available. Generally about 3in. will be found suitable.

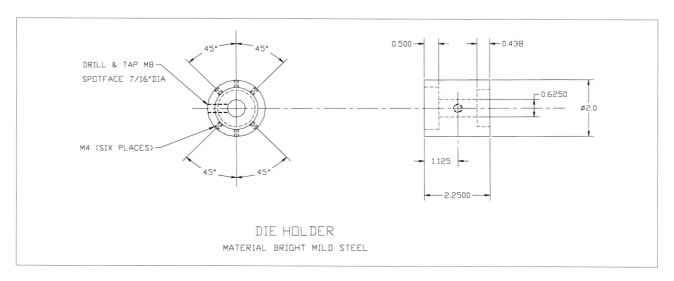

Drawing 3.9

USE

As far as use of the tool is concerned, little needs to be said but, at the risk of boring the knowledgeable reader, a few words of guidance are offered to the beginner. Do take the trouble to ensure that the tailstock is accurately centred before using the tool. It is better to take several cuts than one heavy cut in arriving at the final diameter. Fine threads used in the adjuster screws will make for a more manageable adjusting procedure. Do use cutting lubricant such as 'Trefolex' or 'Rocol R.T.D.' compound which will make your dies last much longer as well as imparting a better finish to the cut thread. Help the die to start the cut by machining or filing a small lead chamfer on the end of the bar to be threaded.

When long threads need to be cut, then they can be produced using the lathe under power. Be sure to engage back gear and the lowest speed. Short thread lengths can be cut by pulling the chuck round by hand with the spindle in neutral if necessary. If using power, adjust the support bar which is held in the tool post so that the die-head drive peg runs out of engagement just as the correct length of thread is approached. The set up for the operations can be clearly seen in the photograph. A point to mention, which is probably obvious, is that the length chosen for the drive pegs should be such that the pegs are able to clear the cross slide when allowed to rotate after disengagement from the support bar.

Another point which I'm sure someone else will be certain to mention if it is not mentioned now, is that ideally the part of the drive peg which contacts the support bar should be flat. The reason for this is to ensure that just before disengagement, any tendency for a round surface (on the peg) to force forward thereby putting an additional side load on the die holder is prevented. The peg in the photograph has not been squared off at the end. I thought I'd just mention it. All that remains to say is clean up all parts and apply chamfers to outer edges.

M.T	B	A	T	t	R	TANG	DIA.	S	X
No1	2.562	0.475	0.375	0.203	0.187	0.343		2.437	0.125
No.2	3.125	0.700	0.437	0.250	0.250	0.531		2.937	0.187
No.3	3.875	0.938	0.562	0.312	0.281	0.719		3.687	0.187

Morse taper shank details

MACHINE VICE FOR THE MYFORD

**Photo 4.1:
Completed machine vice mounted
on Myford vertical slide**

The most serious problem with a temporary work holding arrangement that I used for some time was that its sliding jaw lacked squareness of movement, although sometimes this was a mixed blessing because when holding material which was slightly tapered, the jaw would simply align itself to the work on clamping. The jaw would however end up out of square in the vertical plane. The vice to be described has a tenon and a bottom plate, which now imposes constraints on the jaw movement, keeping all things square. Additionally, a retaining plate has been added to the back of the sliding jaw to keep it in engagement with the end of the screw. Readers owning a mill should have no difficulty in making this little item, but it is also quite likely that being in possession of a mill would mean that they would not need this vice, their need for a vertical slide being rather remote. It would however make a nice little gift for a not quite as well equipped friend! The project is well within the capacity of the Myford lathe and the instructions are aimed at the Myford owner although it is useful as a drilling machine vice.

Drawing 4.2:
Vice body

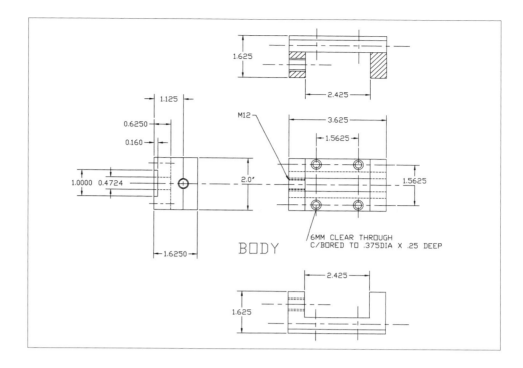

THE BODY

Check the material for sectional squareness and initially choose the flattest side for the bottom. Set up in the four-jaw chuck and lightly true up the surface, which will be the datum for further work. All other surfaces will be either parallel or square to this. Next mark out the hole positions for the four securing bolts and drill through from the newly machined bottom using the drilling machine. Then turn the block over and drill the counterbores to their finished depths. The block can now be mounted on the vertical slide using these fixing holes for machining away the waste material. (Much of this waste can in fact be removed by turning in the four-jaw chuck, which will ease the milling work considerably.) Make sure to set up the vertical slide using a dial indicator so that the block when mounted will be accurately positioned relative to its bottom face. Complete milling of the gap, taking extra care to produce a good finish on the bottom of the gap and the inside of the fixed jaw. An important point when milling, is to clamp up any slides that don't need to move during machining. Another point is to avoid 'climb' milling on the lathe, because most lathes do not have the provision of backlash eliminators.

The long slot needs to be tackled next which will avoid the need to re- set the slide later. This time mount the block using studs passed through from the bottom into

'T' nuts or strips for added strength. Clock up true and set the cutter on centre. I tend to use a wobbler for this job, but a centring needle or a sticky pin will be accurate enough. I used a 12mm end mill for this task, taking light cuts to avoid excessive cutter deflection. When the slot has been completed, follow this up by milling the tracks for the moving jaw bottom plate.

The outer ends can be squared up next. Use parallels under the body to avoid possible damage of slide surface. If preferred, the slide can be swung through 90 degrees and the end to be trimmed allowed to project a little beyond the edge of the slide. It is worth getting

Photo 4.3: Milling the long slot on the underside of the body

the ends square, in the event that the vice might need to be used on end at some point in time.

While set up in this fashion, it is worth drilling and tapping the M12 hole. This thread does need to be axially true in order to avoid alignment problems later that could cause binding of the screw nose with the walls of the hole in the moving jaw.

SLIDING JAW

This part was squared up in the four-jaw chuck, and most of the waste material that would have needed to be removed by milling was roughed out at this stage. In the absence of a milling vice I used the one of the jaws of the newly completed vice body as a small angle plate for mounting the sliding jaw during the next stage of milling. I used a couple of toolmaker's clamps to secure the part in place. Set up carefully with a dial indicator, and check the slot width in order to arrive at the finished width. I used slip gauges for this purpose, and measured across the slip pile with the micrometer, so that the dimension aimed for would be the same. This avoids any errors creeping in from the use of several measuring instruments e.g. a micrometer and a vernier calliper. The length of the tenon was then trimmed back to match the depth of the mating slot in the body. Carefully remove any burrs.

The next stage is to drill the hole in the back of the sliding jaw into which the nose of the tightening screw will engage. The method I used which is by no means the only way to do this stage, is to clamp the jaw into the slot up against the M12 hole. I used a toolmaker's

Photo 4.4: Set up for milling the sliding jaw

clamp for this, then spotted through with a 10.2mm drill. Exchange the drill for a 10mm size and take it down to depth.

SCREW RETAINING PLATE

A small piece of ⅛" gauge plate was used to make this. Cut out the part and file to size. Mark out and drill the three holes. Do not cut the slot into the centre hole just yet. Make a shouldered plug with one end to fit the 10mm hole and the other end to fit the centre hole. This can be turned from any convenient piece of scrap metal, and discarded after use. Push the larger end into the hole in the jaw, and then slide on the retaining plate. The plug will hold the plate so that both holes are concentric. Clamp squarely in position without covering either of the fixing holes, and spot through to transfer the hole positions onto the jaw. The plate can be removed now, and the tapping holes drilled to depth. Tap the two holes. The slot can now be cut in the plate and cleaned up to just fit over the undercut in the nose of the thread.

JAW BOTTOM PLATE

This can also be made of ⅛in. thick gauge plate, as there is just enough thickness to accommodate the countersinking for the screw heads. I made the plate to 1" square. This allows some material to project on either side of the jaw tenon. I decided not to remove the surplus material as it provides a little more margin around the edges of the countersinks. Assemble the jaw into the body, and clamp against the fixed jaw. Using the plate as a template, spot and then drill the first tapping sized hole. Tap to depth, next insert the first screw which will prevent movement while spotting and drilling the second hole. Attach the bottom plate. Clean thoroughly and reassemble. Check the working clearance which needs to be the minimum needed to allow for easy sliding. Adjustment can be made to the working clearance, either by the use of shim, if too tight, or by removing the required amount by skimming in the lathe.

SCREW

I used a length of studding for this part and silver soldered a matching nut on the end. The end was then skimmed over in the three-jaw chuck. A Tommy bar hole was drilled through the nut with a 5.5mm drill. The nose of the screw was then turned to provide a loose fit in the mating hole in the jaw. The extreme end is turned to an angle matching that of the 10mm drill point. The tip is faced off flat. Check fit in the hole to establish the position for machining the undercut. Should the clearance be excessive, there will be more backlash when winding the jaw back. I have allowed the end of the spindle to transfer the thrust to the jaw and added a dab of grease on final assembly.

COMMENTS

The body has been left square all over with the view that it could be useful at a later time where the vice could be used on end, or perhaps on its side. The jaws have been left 'soft'. If at a later time they show signs of deterioration, then they will be faced with harder gauge plate jaws. Apart from these considerations, the vice is very satisfactory, and a useful piece of tooling.

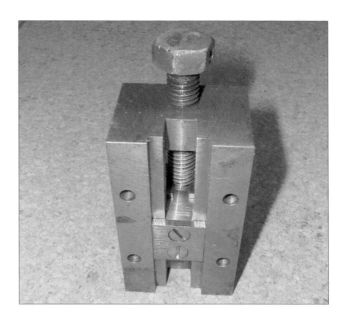

Photo 4.5: Underside view

Photo 4.6: Component parts of the vice

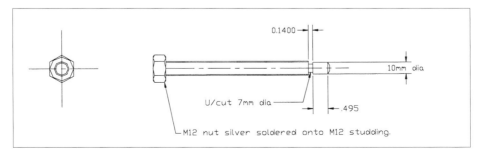

Drawing 4.7: Screw

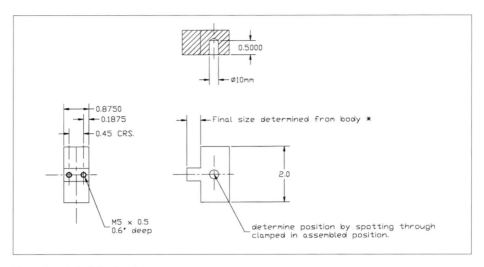

Drawing 4.8: Moving jaw

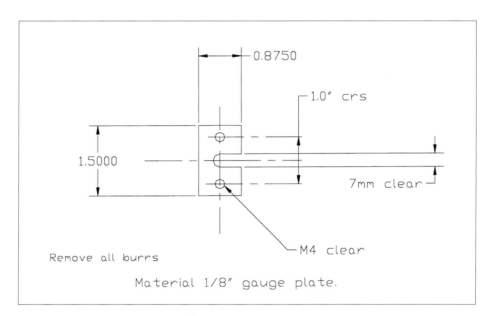

Drawing 4.9: Screw retaining plate

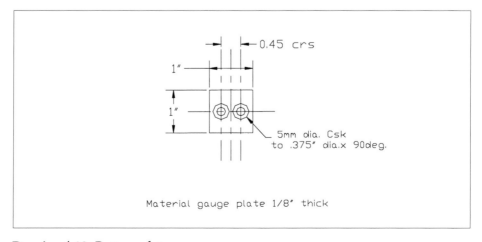

Drawing 4.10: Bottom plate

FLOATING TOOLHOLDER

....

Photo 5.1: Toolholder with collet attachment

Photo 5.2: Set up for die holding

This piece of tooling will accept not only dies, but will also accept taps and small reamers. In order to make this possible, a collet chuck is added to accept the taps and reamers. Inevitably, a series of collets needs to be made to suit the various shank sizes. The tool holding end floats to cater for tailstock misalignment, but a removable sleeve can be slipped into place to lock the floating head in the central position should it be required.

**Photo 5.3:
Turning the Morse Taper**

MORSE TAPER SUPPORT

Face and centre, leaving enough overhang to machine the Morse taper. My part was made to fit a Myford, so should you have a lathe furnished with a smaller size, then don't forget the danger of the bore breaking through the wall of the shank. You might have to make some modifications if this is the case, e.g. drilling a smaller diameter hole.

Take a light skim off the outside diameter with the overhanging end supported on the tailstock. Check that the machined surface is parallel over the full length. Adjust the tailstock if required and re-skim until parallel. Set over the top slide to half the required M.T. included angle.

In the tables, No. 2 M.T has an included taper of 0.5994in. / foot. Half the included taper will be 0.5994/24 = .02497in. per inch.

Set up a dial indicator in the tool post and adjust the dial reading to zero when the top slide has been wound back to a convenient starting position, where the tool tip just touches the work Now advance the top slide forward, a distance of one inch, when the dial indicator should move a distance of 0.025in.. If not then adjust until correct. In theory, the distance moved by the top slide should be slightly greater by about 0.0003in. i.e. 1.0003in..

Check the fit as the turning progresses, by sliding the tailstock into engagement after applying a little high-spot blue to the taper. Traces of the high-spot blue are

evident in photo 5.4. The quality of the fit will become evident well before the final diameter is reached. Make slight adjustments as required, and when satisfied with the result, turn to the final size. I decided against machining a tang onto the end of the shank as it was superfluous in my case, but it may be added, should it ever be required.

Remove the part from the chuck, and after removing the chuck from the machine, clean out the spindle nose taper thoroughly and mount the component directly in the spindle taper. Finish turn the end. Centre drill, drill and ream the hole to depth, and lightly chamfer the mouth of the hole. Drill and tap the M6 hole for the key, which is simply an M6 brass screw, with its end modified as shown.

DIE HOLDER

Set up a length of 1½in. dia. Bar in the three-jaw chuck. Square up the end face, and clean up the O/D. Centre drill the end. Drill and ream to finish at 0.5in.. This diameter needs to have a good finish because the tail end of the collet locates in it. It also provides a concentric datum from which to clock up when reversing to machine the other end.

Turn the diameter to be screw cut back to just short of the shoulder. When the diameter is down to size, finish to length with a squared off parting tool, and turn the undercut at the same time. Next set up the screw cutting tool and set the machine to cut 26tpi. The tool needs an included angle of 55 degrees being Whit form. Do use a screw cutting gauge to set up the tool.

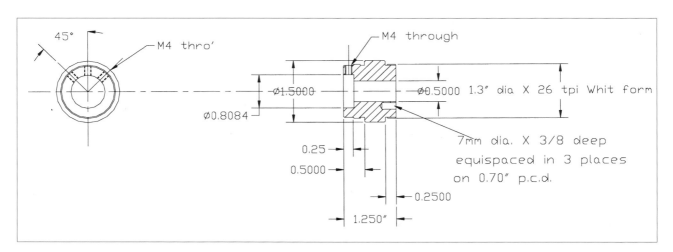

Drawing 5.4: Die holder

It is imperative that the flanks of the thread should end up at the correct angles. If you don't happen to have a gauge handy, then make one from a Whitworth bolt with the same t.p.i. Turn down the head, and remove half the thickness. Hold the in. gauge in the tailstock chuck and offer up the tool to check alignment. Now machine the thread and chamfer the first thread back to clean off the burr. Reverse in the four-jaw chuck and clock true. Face the end to a length to suit your particular die thickness. Bore out the recess and apply a small lead-in chamfer to the bore. Remember that if in your case, the die thickness happens to be greater than the recess depth given in the drawing, then increase the overall length of the die holder by the difference, otherwise the depth of the spring plunger holes may have to be reduced, which will affect the spring loading, and possibly the brass plunger lengths. Next machine the thread for the nose end, and turn the register at the front, long enough to allow for the grub screws to be tapped clear of the thread.

Mark out, centre punch, drill and tap the grub screw holes, which are M4. I used a dividing head to mark out, but because it was too big to set up on the drilling machine table I used a Vee block to support the die holder. Whichever method you use, just make sure that the holes are true along the radius of the part.

Next mark out the three 7mm dia. holes for the brass spring plungers. Drill to depth, (I used a small piece of flat strip as a depth setting gauge for the drilling machine) and chamfer all edges lightly

SLIDING TUBE

Grip the bar at one end in the three-jaw chuck. Face and centre. Drill a 5/16in. dia. through. Check that the centre drilling has not been totally removed, and if this is the case, then re-cut so that the tailstock can be used for support. With the end so supported, take a light skim and check for parallelism over the length. Turn down to the finished diameter aiming for a good finish. Check for a good sliding fit with the support. Machine the inner face of the end flange. Reverse in the chuck (or use the four-jaw chuck if it does not run true) and face the end to leave a flange of 0.125in. +/- .002in.. Turn the flange O/D to size and add the chamfers. Remove from the lathe and check the assembly for the correct clearance. If too much play is evident, then this may be adjusted by carefully removing the desired amount from the mouth face of the screw cup, making certain that the cup is running true in the lathe. Should the clearance be too little, then take the required amount off the flange.

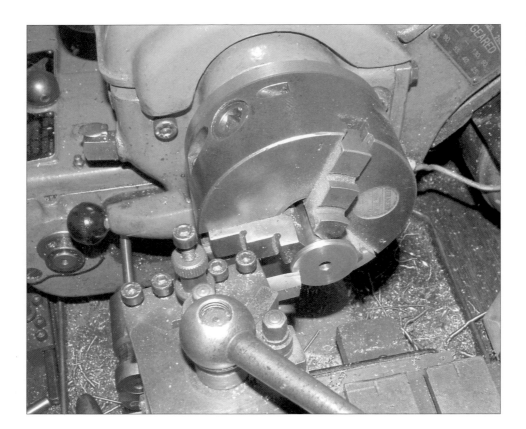

Photo 5.5:
Machining the end faces
of the Sliding Tube

Photo 5.6: Milling the keyway using a vertical slide

Next machine the keyway, using whichever method is available to you. I used a vertical slide lash-up made up of an angle plate to which a spare ML8 cross slide was bolted. The tube is mounted square by using parallels against the back of the vice.

Mill using a ⅛in diameter slot drill.

KEY

This item is made of brass. Either make it from an M6 brass bolt, or make it from scratch. File, or machine the inner end to produce a sliding fit in the keyway. No details are given for making this part.

SPRING PLUNGERS

These are turned from Phosphor Bronze, although brass will suffice. I approached the problem from the situation of first finding suitable springs, and then making plungers to suit the springs. Three are required. Again, these need to be a nice sliding fit in their housings.

RETAINING CAP

Set up the bar in the three-jaw chuck Face and turn the O/D to size. Centre and drill the through hole, and bore in preparation for screw cutting. Back face the

end of the bore and turn the undercut. The back face needs to be finished smooth and square with the axis. Proceed with screw cutting the internal thread, setting up the screw cutting tool accurately as with the male thread. I favour wrapping a piece of plastic insulation tape around the tool shank, and without switching on the machine, advancing the tool into the bore up to the point where it has to be disengaged. I then mark a line on the tape in line with the mouth of the bore. This gives me an indication as to the point where I have to disengage. Carry out trial fitting as the final cuts are approached until a satisfactory fit is achieved. When assembled the two parts should fit with their shoulders butting together. Check the inside gap dimension where the flange of the sliding tube is accommodated. This must be a clearance fit, with not more than 0.005in. of clearance. Clean off any corners with light chamfers.

COLLET END CAP

Machining this part is very similar to that involved in making the retaining cap with some variations notably the register. Turn this dimension as accurately as possible to ensure good location

COLLET

These were machined in the three-jaw chuck. Allow enough to project so that all the turning can be completed in one go, thus ensuring concentricity. Face and centre drill the end. The large end of the collet is furthest from the chuck simply to allow the top slide to be swung away from the machine axis to provide more room, and the same angle setting can be maintained for machining the adaptor insert.

Face the front, and turn the shoulder. Take the O/D down to 0.7in. dia. Use a parting off type tool with the end ground square to turn down the back of the flange as far as the large end of the taper. Follow this with a series of cuts to rough out the recess. Next turn the taper using a left hand tool. The shank end can be turned next, aiming for a close sliding fit in the bore. Take plenty of care with this diameter, as it cannot be tested for fit until after parting off. If you like, it is a good idea to prepare a plug gauge beforehand, and use this as a comparator to finalize the size of the shank. Drill/ream the center hole next and part off.

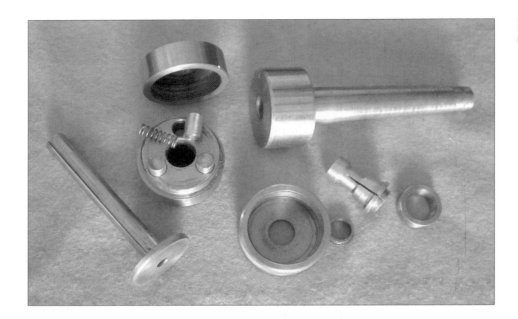

**Photo 5.7:
Collection of components**

COLLET ADAPTOR

The outside diameter of this component is made the same size as that of the dies which are to be used in the holder. The dimension given in the drawing is that of the dies in my collection. Turn the O/D and face the end. Centre drill and drill out the waste from the center. Next bore out to the angle as set. Follow this with the top slide re set to 14 deg. to bore out the rear end. Carefully remove any burrs and part off to size.

COLLET MILLING JIG

This item was made in readiness for slitting the collets and was made from a short length of hexagonal section mild steel bar measuring 1in. A/F. Set up the bar in the three-jaw chuck and turn down the outside diameter to about 0.8in. diameter for a length of around ¾in.. Face and center drill the end. Next drill and ream the bore to ½in. diameter. Taper bore the mouth of the bore to suit the taper on the collet, which will provide

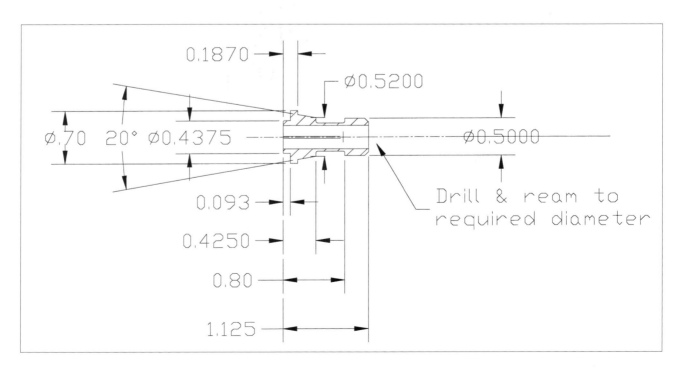

Drawing 5.8: Collet

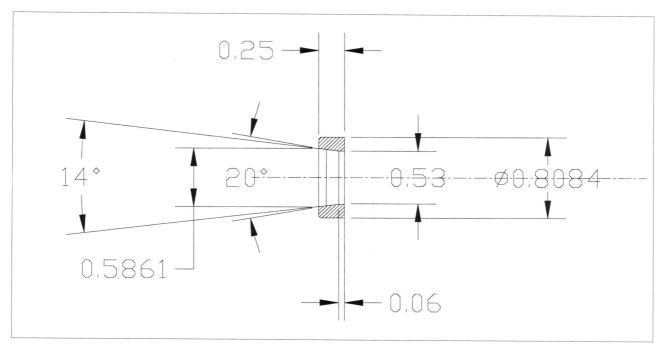

Drawing 5.9: Collet adaptor

additional support for the end of the collet whilst slitting. Finally drill and tap the screw hole making sure that the clamping position corresponds with the middle of the ½in. diameter section of the collet. In use, the jig is set up in the vice mounted on the vertical slide, with the bored end facing front. Clamp the collet into position in the bore. The slitting saw is mounted on an arbor held in the lathe chuck. The saddle is then advanced so that the saw just touches the machined side of the jig. It is then further advanced by an amount equal to half the diameter of the jig plus half the thickness of the saw. The saw will cut the full depth in one cut as long as it is sharp. Don't rush it, but take your time. For the remaining slots, simply rotate the jig by one third of a turn in the vice.

CENTRE LOCKING RING

This part can be made if desired, and simply locks out the floating action. Turn in one setting so that all diameters will be concentric. Remove any burrs with light chamfers. Part off.

ASSEMBLY AND USE

Ideally the faces of the sliding tube should be case hardened and ground, but being without the facility for carrying out these operations, the end face was

lapped on a piece of cast iron, with some fine carborundum lapping paste. The ends of the brass plungers were polished up with some 600 wet or dry paper. All parts were thoroughly cleaned, oiled and assembled. Initially the tool was tested without assembling the key, and no problems were encountered without it. I assembled the key and, satisfied with the ease of sliding the tube into and out of the M.T. holder, I cut another thread. This time, the die holder was released once the die had engaged, and was allowed to feed on its own up to, and against the end face. The lathe was then reversed and the die head screwed itself off, leaving a nicely cut thread. The operation was repeated, with the tailstock deliberately moved off centre by about 0.015in., and the result was another perfect thread. I then tried out the collet to cut a 6 B.A. thread. A 2.3mm hole was drilled through a short length of brass about 8mm in long, but the tap initially had a tendency to slip in the collet. A quick modification was carried out, which meant backing off the internal angle in the insert to 14 deg.. This change tends to ensure that the collet's clamping action is concentrated nearer the mouth. Slipping was eliminated and the next attempt produced a good thread. Collets can be made as and when required to suit the job in hand because they can be made quickly, or made as a set to suit the tools in possession.

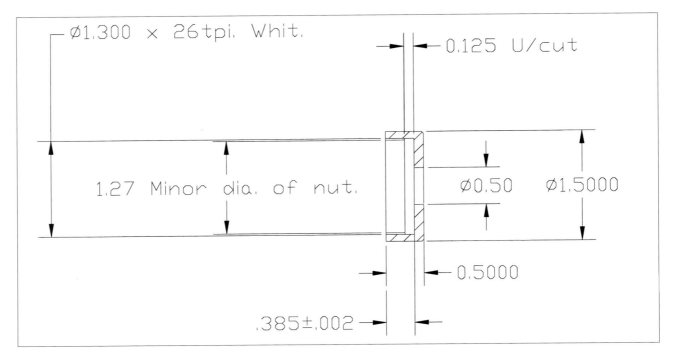

Drawing 5.10: Retaining cap

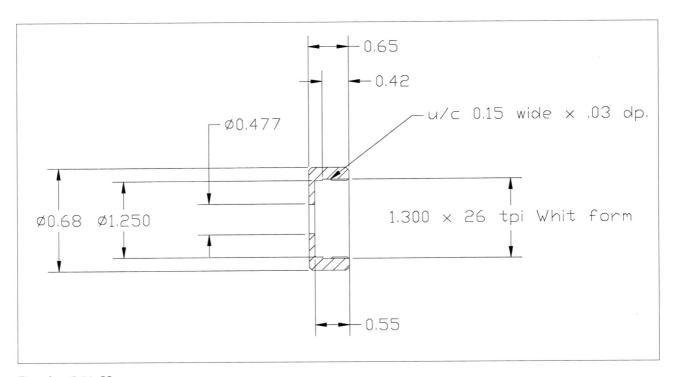

Drawing 5.11: Nose cap

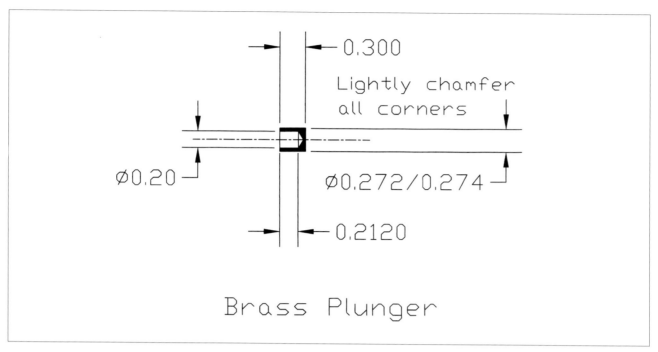

Drawing 5.12: Brass plunger

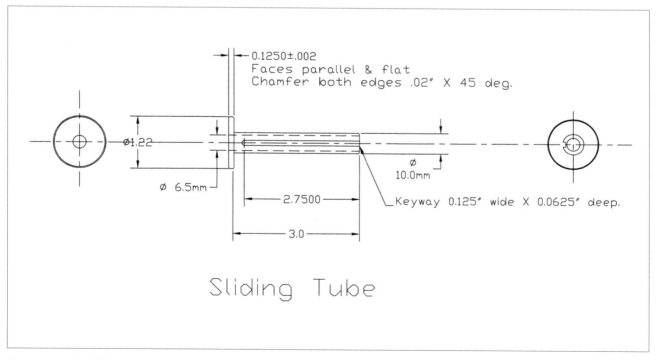

Drawing 5.13: Sliding tube

SADDLE STOP
FOR THE MYFORD

**Photo 6.1:
Completed unit
mounted on lathe**

This item of tooling was made for a number of reasons, quite apart from its obvious usefulness in working to precise lengths and depths, which can be pre-set. It can be used in conjunction with slip gauges, or on its own within the range of its micrometer, which has a 1in. length. One of my reasons for making the stop was simply to machine a relatively long fine pitch thread. Prior to having the bed and saddle reconditioned at 'Myford', I generally found that due to wear and tear on the bed and slides, parts which were intended to end up parallel, always had a slight taper giving rise to problems of fit when these parts were assembled. The threads machined in this little item, fitted perfectly over the entire length without any discernible slack or backlash, which gave me a feeling of satisfaction.

GENERAL DESIGN

The bracket material is mild steel. The dimension giving the centre height of the bore above the bottom edge of the assembly has been increased on the drawings, which has probably been noticed by some readers on one of the photographs. This was done to prevent possible contact of the sliding rod with the joint between the apron and the bottom of the saddle. (I found on a trial assembly that the top edge of the

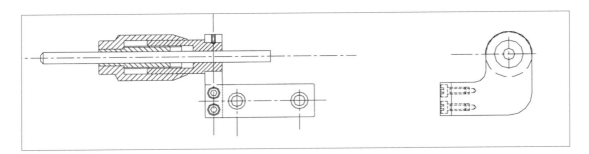

Drawing 6.2: General assembly

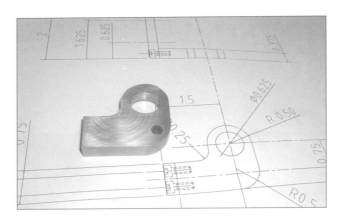

Photo 6.3: Bracket detail

part to be bolted on to the side of the lathe bed had to be lowered to the height corresponding to the top edge of the rack to prevent fouling the saddle.)

BRACKET

This was fabricated from two pieces, a length of 2½in. x ¾in. x ¼in. thick bright mild steel, and the other from a piece of ⅜in. bright mild steel plate 2in. x 2in.. Mark out the thicker part first, centre punch the hole positions and set up in the four-jaw chuck and drill/bore out the barrel-mounting hole. Then follow with the ½in. diameter hole to form the ¼in. radius.

Mark out and drill the holes in the thinner piece, finishing off each hole with a flat bottomed drill or counterbore. Do remember that two of the holes are counterbored on the opposite side to the other. Complete the profile of the thicker part. If, like myself you don't have a milling machine, use the vertical slide, or be masochistic and do it with a hacksaw and file. The extra mystery hole in the thick piece was there because I didn't have another piece without one! I plugged it later. Next drill and tap the M4 grub screw hole.

THIMBLE

I used stainless steel for this part. Turn the O/D to size. Face centre drill and ream right through to size. Drill and bore out the large diameter to give a clearance of about 0.010in. over the barrel. Turn the taper on the end and do not leave a sharp edge, but leave a flat of 0.02in.. Reverse in the chuck and turn the other end. Chamfer any sharp edges for comfort. At this point do not drill and tap the M4 hole for the sliding rod clamping grub screw. This is done later when the brass insert is installed in position. The grub screw will then prevent any movement of the insert relative to the thimble should the fit be insecure. If this is the case, a spot of *Loctite* retainer should help.

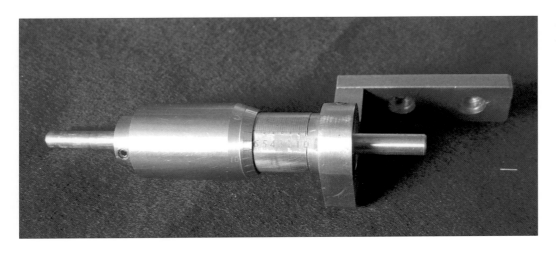

Photo 6.4: Assembled stop

BARREL

It is worth trying out the fit between the stop rod O/D and the reamed hole into which it is to be mounted. To do this, simply drill and ream a ¼in. diameter hole in a bit of scrap and try the stop rod in the hole. If satisfied, carry on. The barrel was made of stainless steel also. Mount the bar in the three-jaw chuck, face and centre. Turn the outside diameter to size. Drill and ream through to ¼in. diameter. Bore out to 0.472in. diameter. Bore out an undercut of 0.510in. diameter for the last .25in. length of the bore to provide a run out for the screw cutting tool. Set up the machine to cut 40tpi. and set up the tool with the same degree of care as with the external screw cutting tool. Move the tool gently into the bore until it touches the end face, and back off 0.2in.

Mark the depth on the tool shank with a felt tip pen. I tend to wrap a piece of plastic insulation tape around the shank and mark the depth on this with a ballpoint pen. Take the first cut and listen carefully as well as watch the line. The hiss of the tool will stop abruptly as the point enters the undercut, at which point disengage. Proceed until a depth of cut of 0.016in. is reached. Take a few extra cuts at the same setting to take the spring from the tool. Chamfer the leading thread. Move the tool out of the way, and using a fine scrap of wet and dry paper wrapped around a drill shank, run it carefully into and out of the bore a few times to remove any trace of roughness from the crests of the thread. Re-mount it in the four-jaw chuck with the other end projecting, and turn the shoulder to a good fit in the bracket. Clean the thread thoroughly removing all residue of swarf.

THREADED INSERT

Brass was my choice for this component with the view that it will provide smooth operation. Set up in the chuck with about 2¼in. projecting. Face and centre drill, followed by drilling and reaming a ¼in. diameter hole right through. Turn the shoulder to provide the interference fit referred to above. Then clean off the O/D to 0.496in. This will give a slightly truncated thread. Sharpen the screw-cutting tool carefully, paying attention to the angle and clearances. The helix angle is small, being of the order of 0.9 deg. So a clearance angle of say 3 deg. would be fine at the leading edge.

Photo 6.5: Machining thimble

Set up the tool with the use of a screw-cutting gauge and machine the thread, using the barrel as a gauge as the final depth is approached. When the barrel shows signs of fitting, clean the thread thoroughly and lubricate. An old toothbrush is useful for the job of cleaning the thread. Retry the fit. Increase the depth in small increments, cleaning after each tool pass, until the barrel screws home. Press the brass threaded insert into position in the thimble, and then drill and tap the M4 tapped hole through both components into the centre hole. If the quality of fit between the two is not as secure as it needs to be, then apply a spot of *Loctite* retainer before assembly, but allow the *Loctite* to harden before cutting the 4B.A. thread in case the wet *Loctite* makes the tap seize in the hole.

Photo 6.6: Machining barrel

Photo 6.7: Screwcutting operation on the insert

GRADUATIONS

Graduations on the thimble were straightforward in so far as the twenty-five division lines were concerned. The top slide was set over to the same angle as for the taper. A tool was ground up with a point angle of about 20 degrees, and the feather edge at the point was honed off with a slip stone. This was to help to maintain the tip quality throughout the engraving procedure. The 25 divisions were obtained using a Radford type dividing head off the bullwheel, which, having 60 teeth, meant indexing 2 turns plus another 24 holes on a 60 hole circle. Another hint to maintain the tool tip in a useable condition, is to grind it without any top rake at all. I found that the top rake angle, if present, caused the tip to hook under the chip at the end of the cut, and caused breakage of the tip. The absence of any rake allowed the point an easier exit from the cut. I cut each line 0.1in. long with a groove depth of 0.003in..

Every fifth line was made 0.15in., which corresponded with the numbers 0, 10, 20, 30 and 40. It must be stated that I had some difficulty marking the numbers for which I had to use an engraver of the type used to make dog tags. My dog would have turned up his nose at any efforts I might have made to provide him with a tag of my making, and I had several attempts, skimming off each one, followed by another try.

BARREL

When faced with the job of engraving the barrel, the lines were engraved using the lead screw hand wheel to advance the cutter each increment of 0.025in. The lines cut to represent the 0.025in. divisions were done using the dividing head. The start and end of each line was thus easy to control, and the lengths of each line are given in the drawing. The numbers became a problem as before, so after just one attempt I decided to do a bit of experimenting using a printer. Earlier in the day, I had been to the local recycling depot with a trailer full of hardcore. I remembered noticing a quantity of computer junk in the skip reserved for electrical equipment. I therefore went back down, and, with the supervisor's blessing, came away with a discarded Panasonic printer that was equipped with a needle printing head. Amongst the relics of my teaching days, I had a few sheets of wax stencils used for typing master copies of student handout notes. These were used on a Gestetner printing machine. Although these were cut on old-fashioned typewriters, it should also be possible to use them on a needle printer. I experimented with differing font sizes and found that the 10-point Times New Roman font, had exactly the same spacing as the linear scale on the

Photo 6.8: Set up for marking the graduations

Photo 6.9: Numerals produced by etching process

barrel, each digit being spaced from the next by 0.1in.. Further trials at etching a suitable scale are shown on a sheet of stainless steel. The electrolyte used was the same as that used for security marking and should be available from *Pryor*, the metal number stamp manufacturer. The barrel was mounted in the vertical slide, and my previous attempts were milled away. The surface was then polished, and the numbers etched on. Although not perfect, the result was better by far than my previous free-hand method.

ASSEMBLY

The bracket needs to be attached carefully to the lathe bed to ensure alignment with the bed. Another important point to observe is that the upper edge of that part of the bracket to be screwed to the bed does not end up above the top edge of the rack. If it does, then the saddle will foul against the bracket. I inserted slips in between the bracket and the underside of the shear, and held the lot together using a toolmaker's clamp. The tapping sized holes were then drilled with pistol drill.

The bracket was removed to open up the holes to clearance sizes, and the holes in the bed were tapped. The assembled stop was screwed into place and the work was complete.

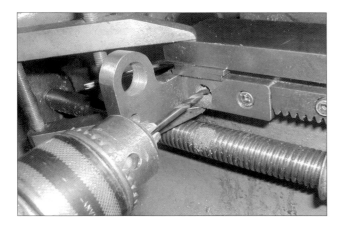

Photo 6.10: Drilling the bed using the bracket for positioning holes

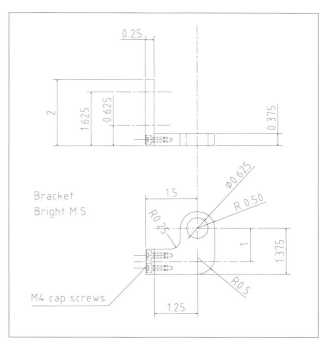

Drawing 6.11: Bracket sub assembly

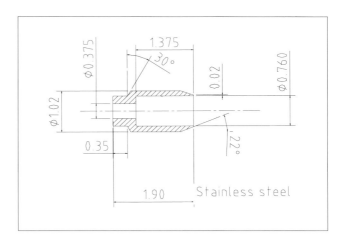

Drawing 6.12: Thimble

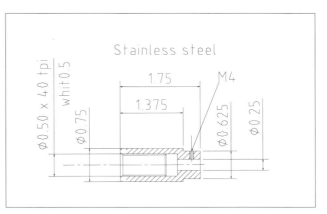

Drawing 6.13: Barrel

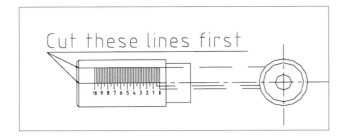

Drawing 6.14: Graduations

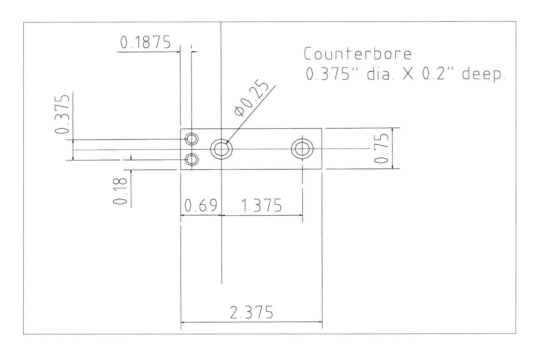

Drawing 6.15: Bracket Plate

MILLING HEAD FOR THE MYFORD LATHE

**Photo 7.1:
Milling Head and
drive arrangement**

The decision to make a milling head came about after beginning to make a dividing head to the 'Radford' design. I realised that I could not machine the worm using my lathe's existing screwcutting facilities. I needed a new quadrant together with a couple of gears in order to cut the required pitch. I made a couple of bids for the bits and pieces on the Internet, and bought a quadrant which was described as being for the 'Super 7 and brand new' but after receiving it I found that it needed work done on it before it would be useable. The 'brand new gear' was bored 0.030in. off centre, so it had to be bushed, re-bored and a new keyway cut in it. The decision to make my own gears was duly born, although I suppose I could have bought perfect items

directly from Myford. The means by which I could cut my own gears, with a modification to mount a drill chuck on the end of the spindle would make the device even more useful, although this extra facility was left until after the first flycutting trials had been carried out. My reasoning for this was due to the long distance between the cutter and the head. This I thought might give rise to problems of 'chatter' caused by the long overhang. Should this be the case, the next step would be to fit an overarm support, which would require a bearing to be fitted on the end of the spindle at the point where the chuck would otherwise be fitted.

The next step was to empty out my scrap boxes on to

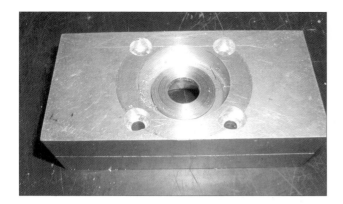

Photo 7.2: Aluminium end housings

the workshop floor to see what was available. The various off-cuts yielded almost all the material needed, and the drawings were duly made up.

END HOUSINGS

These were made from 2in. x ½in. aluminium, each 4in. long. They were bolted together by drilling through the positions, which would eventually be cut away as scrap. Marking out was done on one piece and centre punched accurately. Next drill the bolt hole positions and set up the parts (still bolted together) in the four-jaw chuck, with the centre hole position accurately placed for drilling the centre clearance hole. Use parallels between the work and the chuck face to set up, not forgetting to remove them before machining or they could become missiles! Drill the hole slightly under size, then bore or ream to finish so that the bore can be used later for clocking up prior to boring out the bearing housings. The other boltholes can be drilled in the drilling machine. Counterbore the holes so that the bolt heads are slightly sub flush to avoid interference with the bearing clamping flanges.

Photo 7.3: Removing waste material

Photo 7.4: Milling shoulders to size

Most of the waste can be removed from the plates by sawing, either by hand, or by hacksawing machine (photo 7.3).

BODY

This was sawn just over length and mounted in the four-jaw chuck to face the end. It was then reversed and accurately centred to face the other end to the finished length. (This length is determined by the requirement to mount the spindle either horizontally or vertically when the device is fixed on to the vertical slide, the bolt down holes thus having the same pitch in both planes.) The ends were drilled and tapped M5 so that a disc made to fit the clearance hole in each end plate could be screwed onto each end in turn. The appropriate end plate can then be located on the disc, and the mounting holes spotted through. This procedure would ensure that the two end plates would be aligned accurately on assembly. The spindle clearance hole is then drilled to the final diameter in easy stages.

Next separate the two plates, and using the four-jaw chuck, set up carefully so that the mounting faces are parallel with the chuck face, otherwise the bearings will not be axially true with each other when assembly is carried out. Bore the bearing housing in each end plate.

The bearings are angular contact types 7201 and 7003. These were chosen so that some end thrust could be accommodated should the spindle be used as an

Photo 7.5: Drilling the body

auxiliary drilling head. The end plates can now be finished by machining away the waste, and drilling the mounting holes.

BEARING ADJUSTER NUTS

These were turned from brass and are worth making before turning the spindle as they can then be used to trial fit with their mating threads when screw cutting the spindle.

SPINDLE

Turn from a length of 20mm dia. steel 10in. long. Face and centre both ends and set up between centres. Lightly skim the O/D and then rough turn one end. Finish turn the bearing location carefully followed by the remainder of the end. Set up for screw cutting the 26 t.p.i. thread.

Photo 7.6: Spotting through to locate mounting hole positions

Photo 7.7: Spindle and bearings

When screw cutting between centres, ensure that the driving dog cannot rattle about by tying it if necessary. Turn a small undercut at the run out end to avoid interference when the adjusting nut is assembled. Follow by reversing the part and machining the opposite end. The outer end of the spindle was turned down to 0.5in. diameter and not screwcut at this stage because I wanted to try the device without the provision of an overarm support. Modification at a later stage could be considered after trials. Cross drill and ream the cutter mounting hole and drill and tap the cutter-clamping hole in the end holding the work in the three-jaw chuck.

The last job on the spindle is to machine the keyway in the opposite end. The vertical slide is used, the part being held in the milling vice with a parallel behind it. Incidentally, if no wobbler is available, centre the cutter by marking the upper edge of the shaft with a felt pen. Position the cutter above the shaft, start the

Photo 7.8: Cross drilling the spindle

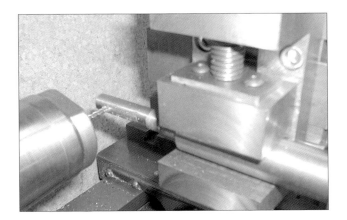

Photo 7.9: Milling the keyway in the shaft

lathe, and raise the vertical slide until the cutter just marks the pen line. Move the saddle back out of the way, add the cutter diameter to the shaft diameter and raise the vertical slide by half this amount.

A wobbler was used to centre the slot drill and for safety, when milling, clamp all slides, which don't need to move.

PULLEY/FLYWHEEL

The pulley is machined on the side of the flywheel. A flywheel is necessary when machining in interrupted cuts to give an improved finish to the work. It stores energy during the part of its rotation when not actually cutting, and then delivers this energy to the work by virtue of its increased inertia. The blank was set up in the three-jaw chuck and cleaned up. The vee forming the pulley was machined on the side, and the mounting bore was drilled and reamed to 0.375in. dia. The pulley was left in the chuck to cut the keyway.

Photo 7.10: Keyway cutting

Photo 7.11: Boring bearing retaining flanges

A .125in. wide parting off tool was set up as shown in 7.10 and the cut was made by advancing the tool using the saddle hand wheel. This method proved to be entirely satisfactory.

BEARING RETAINING FLANGES

These were turned from 2in. diameter aluminium. Discs were cut thick enough to allow cleaning up on the end faces. The depth of the projections indicated with a star on the drawings, are decided by measuring the distance from the end face of the respective bearing to the face of the end plate. Add about .015in. to this dimension so that on assembly, the flange will give a positive clamping force on the bearing. The outside diameter of the projection will also provide a location when spotting through the mounting holes when offered against the respective endplate. The holes are drilled and tapped M5.

Photo 7.12: Turning jockey pulley blanks

JOCKEY PULLEYS

These were turned from 2in. diameter aluminium bar. Two discs were sawn off the bar and faced to thickness. Each was set up in turn in the three-jaw chuck and the centre clearance holes drilled and reamed (to suit an arbor to be used for mounting the two parts in the lathe simultaneously after the bearing housings had been bored). When mounted on the arbor, the grooves were turned in each O/D in turn and de-burred. The bearings were retained in their housings by the application of a little *Loctite* retainer 601 which is more than adequate to hold them in place.

JOCKEY PULLEY SPINDLE

This is an easy turning exercise, which will not need much describing if the flats are to be machined in the lathe. It is worth drilling the centre hole after machining the first flat. When the part is reversed to machine the second flat, set up the newly machined flat, against a parallel. Take care when turning the ball race journal diameters. The ball races can be used to try the fit as work progresses.

PULLEY SUPPORT BLOCK ASSEMBLY

The support block is made from a 2in. length of 1 3/16in. x 5/8in. bar. Set up in the four-jaw chuck, face and centre the end. Drill and tap the M6 hole. Turn

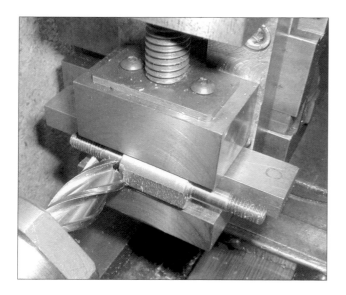

Photo 7.13: Milling the first flat on the spindle

Photo 7.14: Pulley support arrangement

down the 9/16in. diameter. Change to the 3-jaw chuck, face and centre the other end. Drill and tap the M6 hole deep enough to break into the 5/8in. hole when this is machined later. Turn off the corners to give the part a little aesthetic improvement. Purists might prefer to machine the 5/8in. diameter hole before drilling and tapping the hole in from the end, simply to avoid the interrupted cutting action, which can spoil the surface finish inside the large hole. The support flange is made from a length of 3in. diameter steel bar to finish at 2in. long. Face one end, reverse, face and centre the other end. Drill out the waste and bore to accept the column for which I used a length of 5/8in. mild steel bar. Turn the 1.5in. diameter and chamfer the exposed edges. An M8 hole is machined through one side for the clamping screw. Mark out the three 8mm clearance holes on the base of the flange. Centre punch the positions and drill.

MOTOR PULLEY

This is turned from an aluminium bar end. Turn two grooves of different diameters, drilled and reamed to suit the motor shaft. A tapping is made through the side wall to accept a grub screw. No other details are given for this part. They will largely depend on the motor available to the individual constructor.

SPRING DETENT

This is made from steel, and needs to be mounted on a pin turned on the end of a bolt fitted inside the front of the headstock casing. The detent must not have any play, or backlash when engaged with the back-gear for obvious reasons. The spring holding it in contact with the gear needs to be strong enough to prevent the detent from climbing out of engagement.

SETTING UP AND USE

In the assumption that assembly has been straight-forward without any hitches, it might be useful to describe the setting up of the system.

I needed two 30-tooth gears both with 20 D.P. A lump of brass was duly found and turned down to the required outer diameter. To calculate this diameter, add 2 to the number of teeth required, and divide this sum by the Diametral pitch

i.e. $$\frac{(30+2)}{20} = 1.6in$$

The root diameter is obtained by subtracting 2 from the number of teeth required,

Then dividing this figure by the Diametral pitch.

i.e. $$\frac{(30-2)}{20} = 1.4in$$

The depth of cut is therefore half of the difference, being:

$$\frac{(1.6-1.4)}{2} = 0.1in$$

The flycutter used was ground from a worn out centre drill with a ¼in. diameter shank. Care must be exercised in grinding to get the flank profiles correct with sufficient clearance. I used a changewheel from the lathe to copy, using a microscope to check the match.

The spindle is set up on the vertical slide, and set up squarely in both axes using a dial indicator. The motor and jockey pulley bracket are attached to the workbench so that the belt runs smoothly without any tendency to jump off. The belt recommended by Tom Walshaw in his book, "Milling Operations in the Lathe", is leather. I found no difficulty in buying one. The sewing machine shops stock them for the older treadle sewing machines. A leather worker, who I happened to visit previously during my search for a belt, advised me, that when I obtained a belt, to soak it in linseed oil overnight before use so that it would

Photo 7.15: Setting the cutter central to the work

become more pliable, and increase its durability. Check the rotational direction of the spindle before finalising the motor position to avoid the danger of 'climb cutting'.

Next the cutter has to be set up in the spindle squarely to make sure that there will be clearance on both flanks. This can be checked using a square off the lathe shears, and viewing with a good light source. The cutter then has to be set up exactly above the centre line of the work piece. I find that a finely pointed setting needle held in the tailstock is good for this job. The needle has to be concentrically ground, and the tailstock needs to be on centre.

The needle is offered up to the end of the cutter, and the distance from the edge of the cutter to the needlepoint is adjusted so as to be the same from both sides. The cross slide is then clamped tightly enough to prevent wandering out of position during machining. When you are satisfied that all is well and the detent lever is securely in position, advance the rotating cutter to a position just above the blank, and lower it gently to just touch the surface. Move the saddle back to clear and lower the milling spindle by 0.1in.. (I found that the full depth could be machined without problem.) Engage the screw-cutting lever and feed in using the leadscrew hand wheel. The number of teeth to be cut in my case was 30, so the next cut was made after moving the bull wheel round by two teeth. Continue in this fashion until all teeth have been cut. The bores are then machined and the gears parted off. Photo 7.16 shows the completed gears.

The cutting action was found to be smooth and free from 'chatter', and the fitting of an overarm was postponed. A drill chuck has now been fitted which adds to the versatility of the setup. Details of the machining involved in the fitting of the drill chuck will vary according to the type of chuck available. The one used for this modification is a Rohm chuck salvaged from a discarded pistol drill. The thread was 0.375in. x 20tpi with a short register. Screwcutting and turning of the register must be carried out between centres.

Photo 7.16: Finished pair of 30 T gears

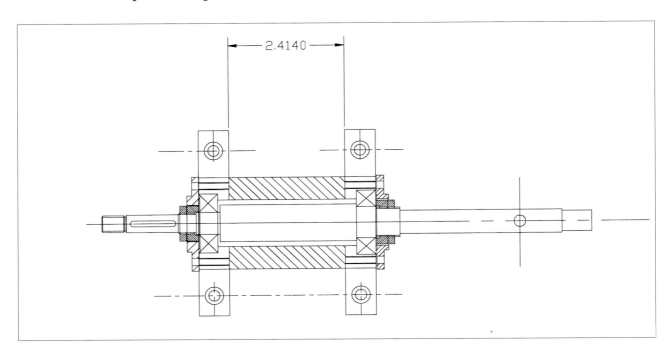

Drawing 7.17: Assembly of the head

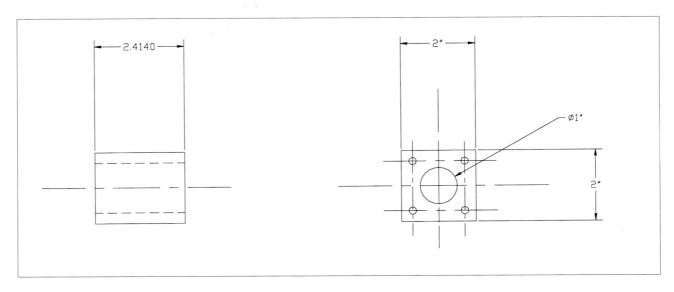

Drawing 7.18: Body

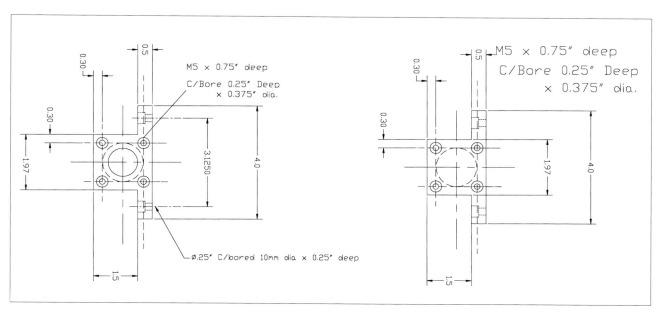

Drawing 7.19: End plate

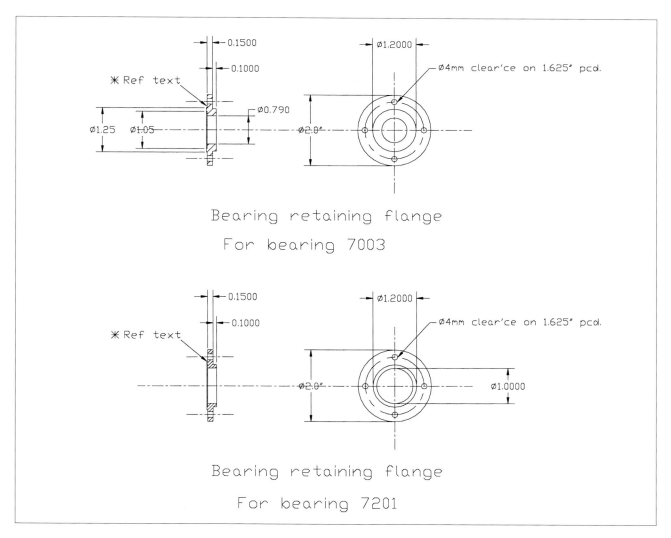

Bearing retaining flange

For bearing 7003

Bearing retaining flange

For bearing 7201

Drawing 7.20: Bearing retaining flanges

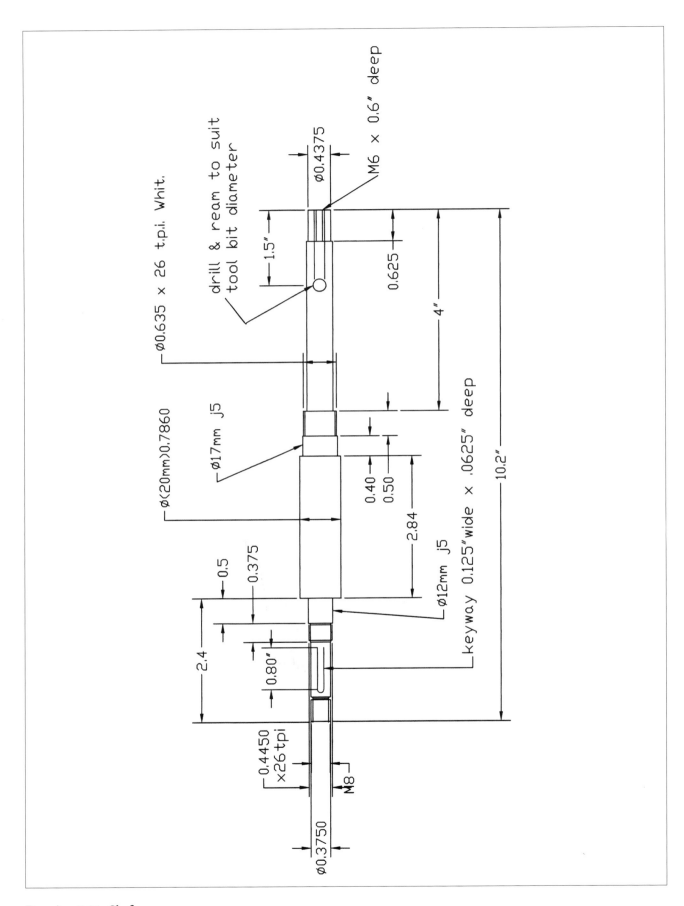

Drawing 7.21: Shaft

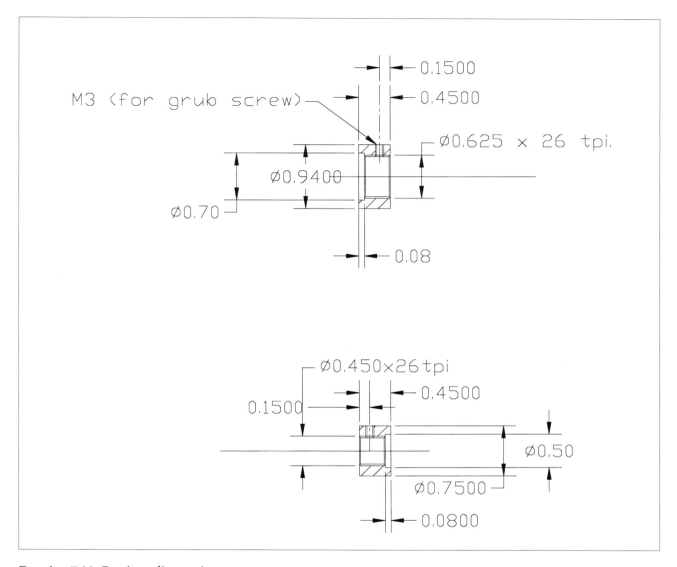

Drawing 7.22: Bearing adjuster rings

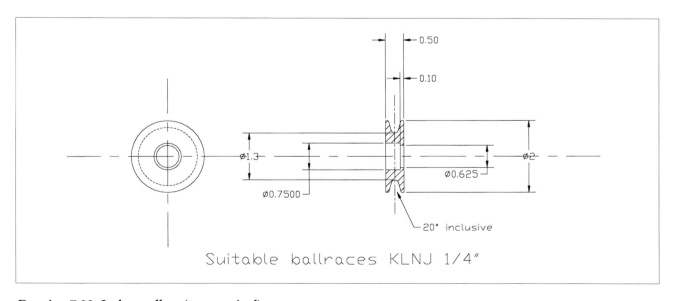

Drawing 7.23: Jockey pulleys (two required)

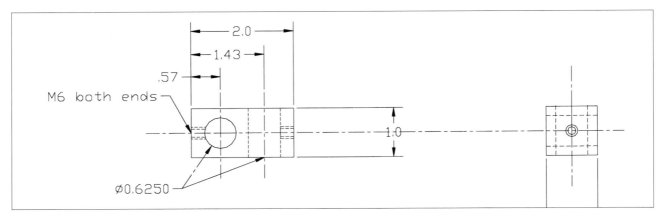

Drawing 7.24: Support block

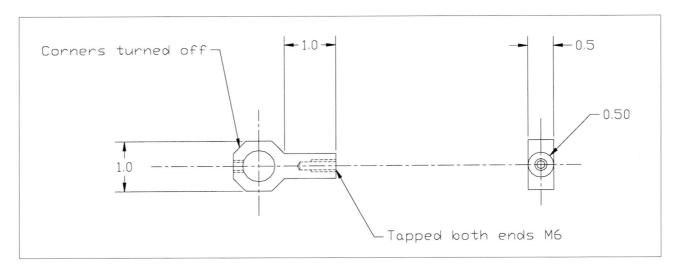

Drawing 7.25: Jocket pulley support block

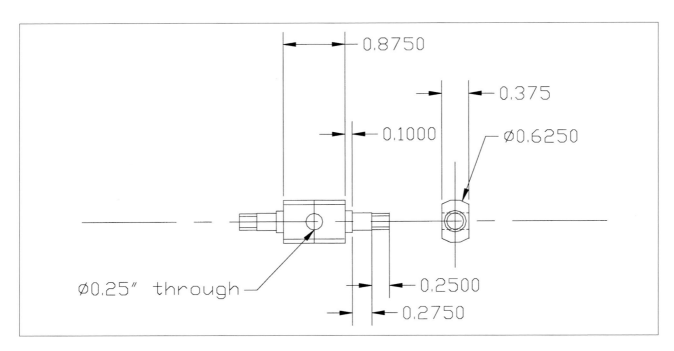

Drawing 7.26: Axle

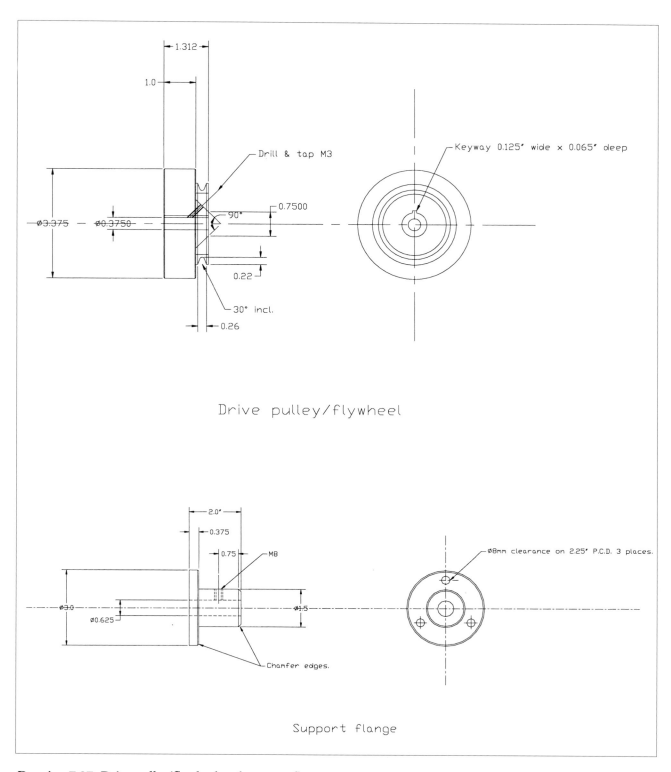

Drive pulley/flywheel

Support flange

Drawing 7.27: Drive pulley/flywheel and support flange

COLLET CHUCK
FOR THE MYFORD LATHE

**Photo 8.1:
Collet chuck
mounted on lathe**

Having moved house to a property which lacked a workshop/garage, and to ease the temporary storage problem, I sold my old Drummond 'M'. This was replaced by a Myford Super 7 B, with the result that I lacked the bits of tooling previously made for the Drummond. In my scrap box I had several Clarkson Autolock milling collets, and decided as my first project to make a milling chuck to fit these collets and save myself some time in getting up and running. The initial intention was to make a set of collets, but because the collets all had 20tpi threads, although of different diameters, the taps might be difficult to

source. I decided therefore to buy the remainder of the collets to complete the set rather than making collets of a different kind. A collet chuck is desirable when holding milling cutters i.e. slot drills or end mills. Holding them in the lathe chuck leads to excessive deflection, a poor finish, and possible breakage, and the problem gets worse the smaller the milling cutters become. I made some sketches to determine the sizes of the parts to be made, and after a rummage in the box of bits and pieces I found some suitable bar ends of En32, and after thinking over the job, I decided to machine the 1.125in. X 12tpi. threaded end first, so that the body

Photo 8.2: Machining body

could be mounted directly on to the machine spindle for machining the other end. This thread could, of course, be machined to suit a different lathe.

BODY - SPINDLE END

Cut the bar to an overall length so as to allow cleaning up to 3in. Mount in the three-jaw chuck, face, centre drill and skim off the outside diameter to clean up. Drill out as much waste as possible to a depth of about 1.2in. to reduce the work involved in boring. The bore should end up at 1.000in. dia. which is the theoretical core diameter of the thread plus half the calculated depth of thread plus a couple of thou' for clearance. This will give the machined thread a truncated inside diameter, which is usual practice on single point cut threads. My usual method in cutting internal threads is to set the tool using a screw-cutting gauge, and then advance the tool manually up to the end of the bore. Touch the end of the bore and back off a touch. Use

the screw-cutting tool to machine the runout counter-bore, making it 0.1in. X 0.06in. deep. This will provide enough runout length to avoid crashing the tool against the end face of the bore! A further safety measure is to mark the tool shank at a point opposite to the mouth of the bore when the tool is up against the end face. I usually wrap a small piece of plastic insulation tape around the tool shank, and mark a line on it with a ballpoint pen, as I find that felt tip markers tend to smudge during the application of cutting lubricant. The idea is to disengage the half nut just as the line comes into line with the mouth of the bore. You have a choice as to the method used in advancing the tool point into the cut. The method I use is to set over the top slide to half the included angle of the thread i.e. half of 55 deg. namely 27.5 deg. The cut is applied using the top slide only, but increasing the tool travel to compensate. If the depth of thread required is 0.053in., then the top slide travel will have to be:

$$\frac{0.057 in.}{Cos 27.5} \quad \text{i.e.} \quad \frac{0.057}{0.887} = 0.064 in$$

In order to check the fit, unscrew the chuck, without removing the workpiece, and offer the thread up to the spindle. If still tight, then replace the chuck on the spindle, and take another small cut. Check the fit again. Continue until a satisfactory fit is achieved. Next, change the screwcutting tool for a boring tool, and bore out the register, checking the fit as before. Before removing the body from the chuck, chamfer the mouth of the bore lightly. If happy, then remove it from the chuck and set aside until the collet holder has been made.

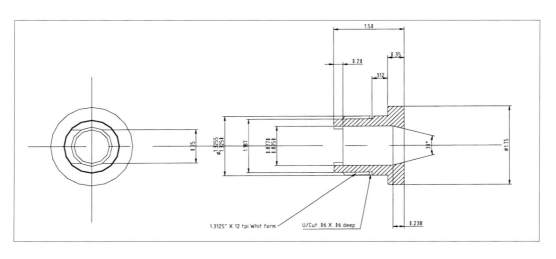

1.3125" X 12 tpi Whit form   U/Cut .06 X .06 deep

Drawing 8.3: Collet Holder

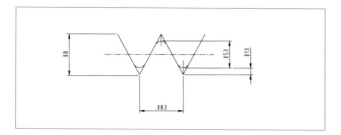

Drawing 8.4: Thread form

COLLET HOLDER

Make this item from a length of steel, which is long enough to allow a secure grip in the three-jaw chuck. Turn down the outside diameter, face and centre the end. Drill out the waste from the centre and ream or bore through to a diameter of 0.75in. I would suggest that the thread is cut next, before the bore is completed, the reason being that screwcutting places quite a heavy load on the component, and if it does move slightly, it would not be disastrous to concentricity, because the bore will eventually be machined true to the finished thread. If the bore is finished first, it can be supported using a centre in the tailstock if necessary.

The thread O/D will be reduced from the nominal diameter of 1.312in. by .026in., which is 2 X (H/6) where H is the maximum depth of thread (0.08in.). Therefore turn the length to be screwcut down to 1.286in. diameter. Turn the thread runout undercut,

but leave the register diameter until after screwcutting is finished for the same reasons as above. Now cut the thread and finish off with a chaser if one is available. Now finish turn the register.

The collet holder bore is tackled next, and needs to be machined such that no radius is left at the start of the taper, which could prevent the collet from seating correctly. The method I used was to set over the top slide to 15 degrees and set the dial to zero. The parallel portion of the bore was taken out to size using the graduated leadscrew dial to arrive at its correct depth. The last and finishing cut in the bore was taken 0.05in. beyond its dimensioned length, and the boring tool was moved back to its correct finished position. (This leaves a small step instead of a radius.) The top slide is now advanced in order to complete the taper in the end of the bore. It can be taken out in one cut leaving a good finish. Machine the chamfers. Photo 8.6 shows the holder with the threads cleaned up, the register finish turned, and the bore completed Do not part off yet as the chucking end can be used to hold the part for milling the recess. This was carried out in my case on the drilling machine using two Myford cross slides bolted together and set up as a milling machine. (Photo 8.8.) Then part off leaving some waste for cleaning up. I left the cleaning up until after the whole chuck was assembled with a slot drill mounted in the collet. Leaving the cleaning until this point means that the face of the collet can be brought out flush with the front face of the holder.

Drawing 8.5: Chuck Body

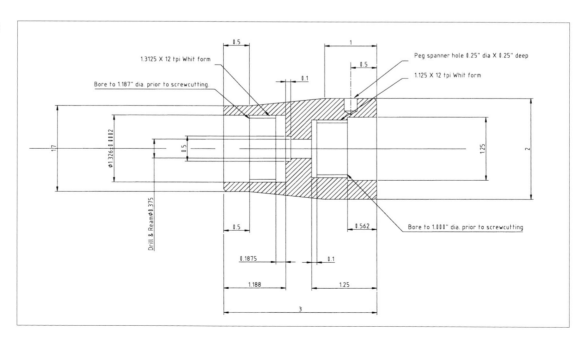

Photo 8.6: Body with threads cleaned up and bore completed

BODY - COLLET END

Before re-mounting on the lathe, it is worth drilling the peg spanner hole, which can be made to suit an existing spanner. Chamfer the mouth of the drilled hole as it prevents the raising of burrs by a slipped spanner!

Remove the lathe chuck from the spindle, and replace it with the body after cleaning out the newly machined thread and the spindle thoroughly. All remaining

Photo 8.7: Milling the slots in the collet holder

turning work on the body can now be completed in the knowledge that when finished, it will be truly concentric with the lathe spindle.

Face to length and centre the end. Drill through, and ream the hole in readiness for the cone centre mounting. Drill out the waste to prepare for screw-cutting to a diameter of 1.212in.. Bore out the thread run-out counterbore and the flange recess counterbore for the cone centre.

Set up for screw cutting as for the other end, but this time you have the male counterpart for checking the fit. Aim for a smooth running fit, which is not too tight, because location will be maintained by the register diameters. After machining the thread to give the desired fit, machine the register in the mouth of the bore, checking the fit using the collet holder.

The outside of the body is mainly aesthetic, given that the wall thickness requires enough material to provide vibration-free rigidity. I aimed for solid design without excessive bulk that could be a hindrance to access when milling certain awkward components. Roughing out the outside of the body can be carried out at this stage if you wish. Don't forget the all important lead-in chamfers. Photo 8.7 shows the finish-turned body viewed from the side.

CONE CENTRE

Make this from steel, which can be hardened, because this component is subject to wear. A piece of silver steel would be fine. All turning needs to be carried out at the same setting, to ensure concentricity. The tool centre height must be absolutely bang on centre height for turning the cone, otherwise the flanks will not be straight. Make the shank a slight interference fit in the bore. Face off the end and set over the top slide to 30°C. Turn the cone and flange. Make the flange a clearance fit in relation to the counterbore. Apply the chamfers and part off. Check the fit in the bore. If you are satisfied that it will enter the bore, there is no need to press it all the way in, as it needs to come out again for heat treatment. If it is silver steel, then it will need to be heated to 770/790°C, and preferably oil quenched to prevent possible cracking by water quenching. Tempering can be carried out in the domestic oven (while the chief domestic all powerful supervisor has her back turned). Holding at a temperature of 200° C should produce a hardness of around 61 Rockwell C. which is hard enough whilst removing any excessive brittleness.

Assemble the cone centre into the body after cleaning mating parts. Mount a suitable milling cutter in a collet and assemble. With the assembled chuck mounted on the lathe tighten the collet holder so as to grip the cutter. Do not use excessive force, but make sure that the cutter is held securely. Examine the relative positions of the collet end face and the front face of the collet holder. The holder can now be faced off flush with the collet and the chamfer put on its outer diameter. A small chamfer can be added later to the mouth of the holder.

A peg spanner hole can be drilled in the holder flange, or if preferred, two spanner flats can be milled. The tool is now complete.

Drawing 8.8:
Cone tool seating

Drawing 8.9:
Collet

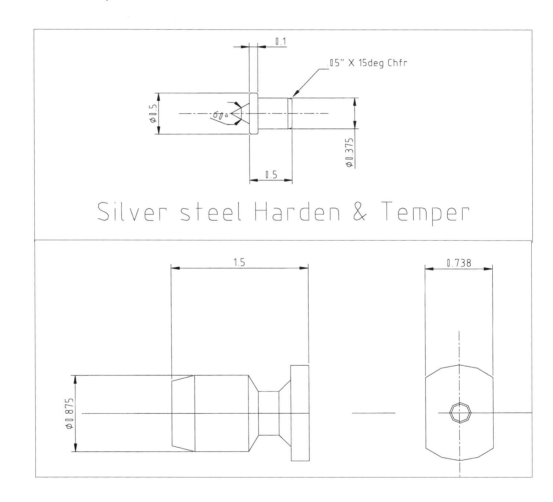

ROTATING CENTRE

Photo 9.1: The completed rotating centre

The possession of a rotating centre makes the turning of many components much easier and often much quicker. This is because they can be finished using higher speeds without the inherent problem of local overheating which can be a nuisance when using solid centres. The cost of a commercially available rotating centre can be an obstacle. This accessory is certainly desirable, if not an absolute necessity, so why not make one? It does require careful and accurate machining, but that is all part of the enjoyment of making your own tooling.

It was decided to make a centre with a No.1 Morse Taper (MT) shank, so that it could be used on my smallest machine. Choose the MT shank, to suit your machine. The races used are standard sizes and will not be difficult to obtain. They are available from most bearing stockists and you should have these items before boring their housings. The bearing part numbers are given below.

THE BODY

This can be turned from a length of decent quality BMS, or a tool steel, the total length being equal to the body length plus whichever MT length is chosen. Grip one end in the three-jaw chuck, with enough protruding to machine the taper. Rough out the taper leaving an allowance for finish turning. The taper is short enough to dispense with the need for tailstock support, provided that the finishing cuts are light. Turn the shank to a parallel section first of all; this will be a help in setting the top slide over to the correct angle for the final taper turning operation.

The method I use most often for setting the top slide is to set up a dial test indicator in the tool post with the plunger resting on the now parallel shank. Set over the slide as accurately as possible to half the included angle.

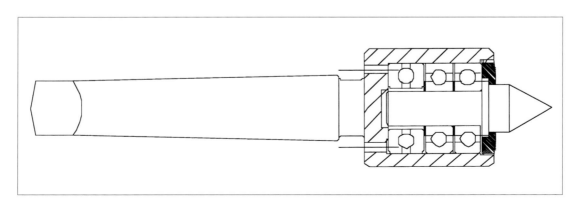

Drawing 9.2: General assembly

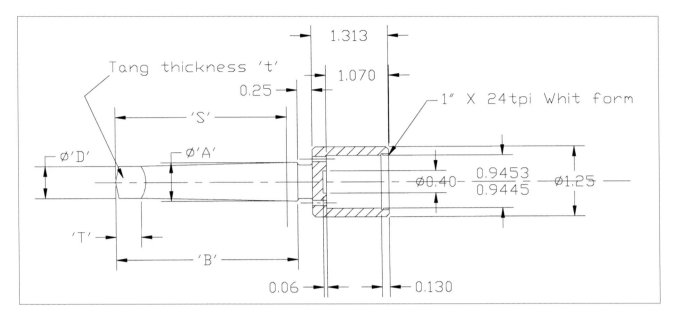

Drawing 9.3: Body

This can be a guess at this stage. Next advance the slide by one inch, and check the dial reading with the taper per inch corresponding to half the included angle. Check the accuracy of fit using a MT adapter sleeve if one is available. This check must be carried out at an early stage, because the tang end will not enter the slot provided in the adapter until flats have been machined to form the blade of the tang. Should your machine not require provision of a tang on the end of the taper, then you can dispense with the tang and turn a short cylindrical end, as shown in the photograph. A tang will be required if it is intended to use a Morse taper sleeve for use in a larger machine. Sizes are given in a previous chapter on the 'Tailstock Die Holder'.

A little marking blue can be used to highlight any high spots, but be sparing in its use. When the correct size is obtained, remove the chuck, and after cleaning out the taper in the lathe spindle nose, mount the newly completed taper in place for all further machining i.e. the bearing housings, retaining collar thread and the outside diameter.

BORING FOR THE BALL RACES

The ball bearings must be measured accurately as this will be the first diameter to be bored to size. Drill out the waste as far as possible, before setting up the boring tool. Rough out the bore to slightly less than the full depth and sharpen the tool before the final cuts are taken. It will help to machine the mouth of the bore to

the final diameter before extending to the full depth, then finish by winding back to the centre in order to square off the end face. (It is much easier to measure accurately at the mouth of the bore than some distance inside; but make certain that if you are using the top slide to bore to depth, that it is not turning taper). Remember that the radius left in the corner must be small enough to allow the bearing to seat properly onto the end face of the bore. There must not be any appreciable clearance between the bearing outer diameter and the inside of the bore. Ideally the bearing should enter with a small degree of interference. The tolerance is small, hence care must be exercised to obtain the correct fit. It is better to keep on the tight side; even if this means removing the last by gnats whiskering with some fine wet or dry abrasive paper with a few drops of oil added.

INTERNAL SCREW CUTTING

When you are satisfied with the bores, then screw-cut the 24tpi thread. The first step is to bore an undercut to allow the tool to run out at the end of the cut. Do not make this too wide, as the effective number of threads left in engagement will be reduced. About 1.5 times the pitch will be about right. The depth of the undercut should be the full depth of the thread.

Set up the screw cutting tool angle accurately using a screw cutting gauge if one is available. Use of such a tool is a boon, as it does provide an aid to the correct engagement of the mating threads If your lathe does not have an automatic disengagement trip which can be set to the required distance inside the bore (which was a very useful feature of my old Drummond M lathe), mark the tool shank to indicate the depth; or put a pencil mark on the bed at the point where the carriage will be when the tool is at the correct depth. Now take a trial cut of about 0.010in., check the pitch with a screw pitch gauge. If all is well take successive cuts until the full depth of thread is reached. It is best to take several cuts at the full depth in order to take the spring out of the tool, and finally chamfer back the first thread. I should state here at the risk of boring the more experienced reader that the screw cutting operation must be carried out at a slow speed, with the back gear engaged.

A REMINISCENCE

Before going on to the next stage, it might be worthwhile mentioning an incident that took place in the apprentice training workshop where I began my apprenticeship. One of the favourite items of equipment we had to make was a milling jack that had a 0.75in. x 20tpi thread in the body. This had to be screw cut in the lathe. One of the lads completed the screw cutting and chamfered the leading thread, but then decided he would finally polish the mouth of the threaded bore with a scrap of fine emery cloth. As soon as he began this last operation, his thumb instantly screwed itself into the bore cutting a 20tpi thread up to his knuckle; which was duly unscrewed by the apprentice supervisor before the lad woke up from his faint. He was, from that day onwards, affectionately known as 20tpi Williams. I reckon that we should all be fairly safe on this little job unless someone happens to have a thumb of about an inch diameter!

BACK TO THE JOB

Lastly drill and tap for a small grub screw to retain the collar in position. Mark out the body for this screw after a trial assembly to make sure that the screw breaks through at or near the centre of the retaining collar. A grub screw of M2 size will be about right for the job.

The tang is milled first, if one is required. Some lathes, my own included, do not require the provision of a tang for ejection. If one is required however, the body

is set up on the vertical slide, mount an end mill in the chuck, take a light trial cut along the underside, check the remaining thickness and mill away the remaining waste material from the other side thus completing the tang.

SPINDLE (SILVER STEEL)

The operation sequence for making this component could be varied according to personal circumstances. I chose to hold the bar initially, at the end which will finally be turned to form the conical point allowing about 1.5in. to protrude. Holding it thus will enable trial fitting of the bearing to be made as the work approaches the correct diameter. It is a good idea to turn the 0.942in. length to about 0.2in. over length initially, so as to provide a trial length for turning the 0.354in. dimension accurately. Once this diameter has been produced to satisfaction, it is then a relatively easy matter to extend this diameter over the remaining length before finally facing off the unwanted extra portion. Next set up a parting tool in the toolpost and position the blade edge so that the 0.069in. dimension is produced a little oversize. Feed in the cutter just short of the full depth and withdraw it whilst maintaining longitudinal position. Measure the flange just made accurately, and index back the top slide to remove the excess thus leaving the correct width. If the parting tool cutting edge is 0.125in. or slightly over, then feed in to depth to produce the 0.5in. diameter. The next step is to reverse the work piece, this time holding it in the four-jaw chuck. Use the dial indicator to set the work to run as true as possible. Next set over the top slide to 30 degrees (60 deg. inclusive). Set up a right hand tool in the toolpost; making certain that its cutting edge is set accurately to centre height. If the setting height is either too high or too low, the flanks of the point being turned will not be accurate. It will be immediately evident that the line of cut will not pass through the tip. Take extra care to obtain the best finish possible so that the part can be easily polished after hardening without loss of accuracy.

HARDENING AND TEMPERING

To harden, heat up gently in subdued light to a cherry red colour, and quench in oil. I find that old engine oil is good enough for this purpose; although other oils are usually specified. If you use old car engine oil for this

**Drawing 9.4:
Centre**

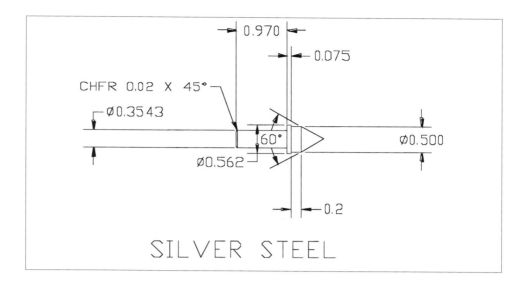

purpose please first ensure that the container is open to the atmosphere for a good period of time to allow any dissolved unburnt hydrocarbons to evaporate off. Maximum hardness will not be obtained unless silver steel is quenched in cold water, but this does entail some risk of cracking, and maximum hardness is not required anyway, as this condition also goes hand in hand with brittleness. A tip when quenching is to plunge the component into the oil as vertically as possible, and quickly. Don't lower it slowly like lowering chips into a deep fryer, especially if the component happens to be lying on its side, as this will increase the risk of distortion and the possibility of cracking.

When the part has cooled sufficiently to be handled, test it for hardness with a small file, say on the end farthest from the point. The file should slide over the surface without removing even a scratch. If this condition has been achieved then polish the part in readiness for tempering.

(Tempering is a process that removes some of the hardness, but not all of it, simultaneously increasing the toughness). As this is a small component tempering directly using a gas torch is a little risky, unless you are particularly adept at it. The problem is that the point is thin and liable to heat up much quicker than the thicker parts. A safer method is to heat up the component in hot sand, which can be heated gently in an old saucepan on the gas stove. Beware of using aluminium pans; they can melt. As the sand is being heated stir the component around in the sand and

watch it carefully for colour changes. The first indication will be a slight change to pale straw deepening in colour gradually. The component should be removed just as it changes to brown. At this stage it can either be allowed to cool in air, or once again quenched in oil, the end result will be more or less the same. Finally polish.

RETAINING COLLAR (MILD STEEL)

A piece of 1in. diameter bright MS bar will do for this component if it is set up to run true. Turn to about 0.995in. dia. in preparation for screw-cutting. Set up the threading tool carefully. If grinding this tool point from a blank, take care to ensure that the point is the correct angle for the thread form being turned (55 deg. for Whit. or 60 deg. for metric). The other thing to watch is that the front clearance angle is ground a degree or two more than the helix angle of the thread, otherwise the tool will rub. The trailing angle can be left square. Screw-cut a length slightly longer than required and test for fit as the depth is approached. If a slight burr has been thrown up at the crests of the thread during screw-cutting, remove it by holding a fine file lightly against it as the machine is rotating, and clean before checking the fit. (I keep an old toothbrush for this job as it gets into the bottom of the threads.) Next centre drill out the waste leaving a little for finally boring to size. Then bore out the 0.625in. diameter recess to a depth of 0.08in.. Finally part off to length. To complete, drill the peg spanner holes to about 0.05in. deep.

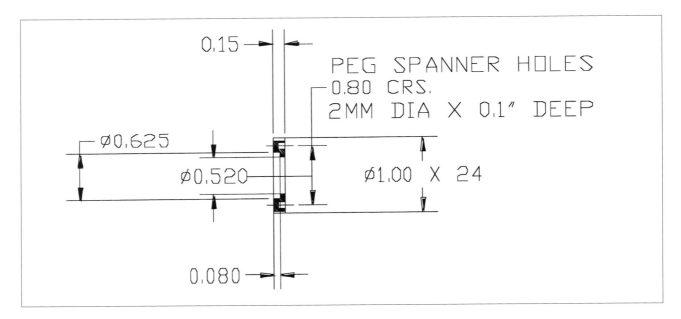

Drawing 9.5: Retaining collar

SHIM WASHERS (MILD STEEL)

Two are required, These are simply turned to the outside diameter, the centre drilled out, and parted off the bar. If the parting tool is well sharpened, there should be no problem from burrs. Clean up the sides by rubbing on an oilstone which will leave them clean and flat if done carefully.

ASSEMBLY

Assemble carefully and on no account use a hammer directly on the bearings. If these are tight, it is worth taking the trouble to turn up a short tube which can be placed against the outer rings of the races, and then they can be gently tapped into place keeping them square on entry. (If a trial assembly was not successful, the bearings can be removed using a ⅛in. diameter length of silver steel passed through one of the holes drilled through the back of the bore, and gently tapped out using each of the holes in turn.)

The position of the retaining collar will have to be checked by measurement of the individual components. Remember to pack the bearings with a little light grease similar to that used for car wheel bearings, as it is a water resistant type. Do not be tempted to pack the grease in so as to completely fill up the space available, too much can cause overheating and short service life. Lastly, assemble the retaining collar, tightening until the spindle cannot be rotated with the fingers. Slacken off about a quarter of a turn and lock with the M2 grub screw, and you are home and dry.

BEARINGS REQUIRED

Thrust race - type 51100 (one off)

Ball races - type RHP 609 (two off)

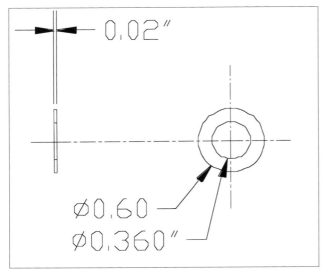

Drawing 9.6: Shim washer

THE CHIPMUNK WOOD TURNING LATHE

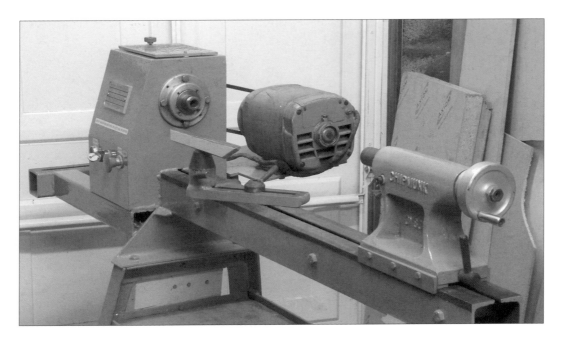

**Photo 10.1:
The Chipmunk
Lathe**

The decision to build a woodturning lathe came after several years of watching the advertisements for a suitable second-hand machine of reasonable quality at a suitable price. Machines tended to be either too flimsy, or, if suitable, too expensive. My aim, therefore, was to undertake the design and construction of a suitable lathe with a specification equalling those available commercially, and by using basic workshop facilities of a centre lathe, drill and an electric welder. The photograph shows the tailstock made using an aluminium casting. The majority of constructors however, lack foundry facilities, and I have substituted a fabricated design for this item. This has a hollow spindle, useful for drilling long holes with an augur, a facility not designed into the cast version.

The machine is made from structural mild steel

sections, all of which are readily available. Some of the construction methods used, may be a little unusual, but are, nonetheless, effective. The maximum distance between centres is 30in. with 11½in. swing over the bed, although it would not be a problem to increase the bed length should it be needed. The swing at the bowl turning end is 17½in. The machine is furnished with both forward and reverse rotation, and the switchgear is 'No volt release'. The headstock is a welded fabrication of rigid construction providing a vibration-free operation that is essential for a good finish. One leg is furnished with a levelling adjuster that caters for any condition of floor. Four spindle speeds are available although there is ample space to provide another range if required. The actual speeds achieved are 470, 900, 1530, and 2665 r.p.m.

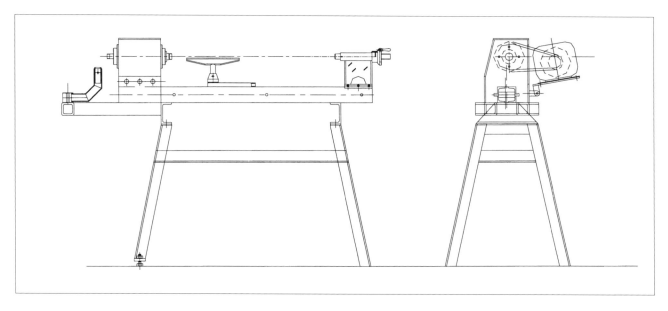

Drawing 10.2: The 'Chipmunk' Wood Turning Lathe - General Arrangement

Material is best obtained cut to size if it is possible, and many stockists operate a cutting service that will help to avoid much backbreaking work with a hacksaw and file. Check the material before purchase to ensure that the channel used for the bed is free from any twist or wind. Much of my material was cut using oxy-acetylene equipment, and some was machine cut.

THE BED

This is the first sub-assembly to be tackled. Clamp the two lengths of channel back to back and check before machining that the edges match over the full length,

Photo 10.3: View on end of bed

trying various arrangements until the best condition is found. Take pains to obtain the greatest degree of accuracy; whilst one may question the need for a high degree of accuracy in the bed of a wood turning lathe, it will be appreciated when drilling holes using the tailstock that a drill which does not enter the work on centre will wander about producing an oversize hole, as well as not following the true centre of the work. Next, mark out the channel on one piece only, then drill and ream through both pieces whilst they are clamped securely together.

BED SPACERS

These are simple turning jobs. Three are required. In order to get the ends concentric with each other, use the four-jaw chuck or turn between centres. Aim for a snug fit without any undue play. Then assemble the bed and check it again for accuracy. It is advantageous at this stage to clean up the top face as true as possible in readiness for the tailstock and hand rest. For this task I used an angle grinder that made the job easy, and it also made light work of bevelling the edges of the other components in preparation for welding. Set the assembled bed aside until later.

BEARING HOUSINGS

I cast the blanks for my machine, at the same time casting the tailstock body, making use of the school foundry. Should you have some aluminium blanks of suitable size, they would be perfectly OK. First turn the outside, leaving out the bores. Then, reverse the work, setting up in the four-jaw chuck, and drill out as much waste as possible. Bore to give a transitional fit with the respective bearing. The fit must be good. Machine the end face on the same chucking to ensure squareness and then bore the clearance hole for the spindle last of all.

The four bolt holes can now be drilled, allowing generous clearance on one housing to aid with bearing alignment on assembly. Drill two extra holes on the P.C.D. of the outer diameter of the bearing, to facilitate bearing removal whenever such an event may become necessary.

HEADSTOCK FABRICATION

Clamp the two end panels together and, after marking out the top plate, drill pilot holes suitable for your trepanning tool or hole saw through both panels. Mark out and drill the bolt holes for the bearing housings. Separate the two plates and machine the centre holes to finished size, working through from both sides of each plate in turn. Clamp the work to the machine table before cutting out, otherwise your work could go into orbit!

Turn two plugs from any suitable material with which to line up each bearing housing with the respective holes machined in the headstock panels. The plugs will centre the bearing housings so that the bolt hole positions can be accurately spotted through, then drilled and tapped. Next, cut out the slot that straddles the bed using the width of the assembled bed to work

to. A good fit here will greatly help in the alignment of the headstock spindle later.

The next stage requires three short lengths of tube of about 2in. diameter (scraps of scaffolding tube would do the trick), the ends of which must be turned square with their axis. The sum of their finished lengths must be equal to the inside dimension measured between the end panels of the headstock.

The panels are now reassembled using a long bolt or stud to hold the panels together, but this time with the tubes in between. Resist at all cost any temptation to use just one tube as a spacer. Consider the effect on your blood pressure when attempting to remove it after welding up the assembly. The whole idea of using the tubes is to ensure that the outer faces of the panels remain parallel after welding, as the bearing housings eventually bolt on to them.

SWITCH ARRANGEMENT

The holes for the switches need to be machined before welding on the front panel. Make certain that the switches you have obtained will allow assembly from behind the panel, because the bed takes up a good deal of the available space inside the headstock, which can make wiring a little tricky. Move the switches up a little if desired, but not too much in case they foul the pulley.

When assembling the headstock for welding, misalignment can be avoided by standing the clamped

Photo 10.4: Headstock with cover removed

Photo 10.5: Electrical switching components

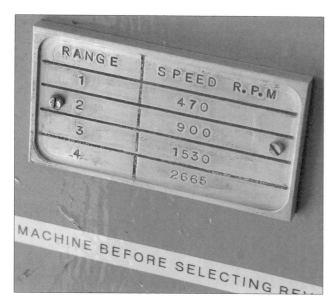

Photo 10.6: Speed range plate

Photo 10.7: Bearing housing and spindle adjustment. Bowl turning end

assembly in place over the bed where it will be eventually welded. Quite obviously, the access holes in both top and rear panels must be cut out before welding. Next, tack the assembly carefully with small welds, after which, if satisfied that all is well, finish welding the whole sub-assembly, balancing weld sequences in order to avoid distortion. The final result should have continuous welds around the outside, with heavy stitch welds around the inside. Remove the studding and knock out the centre tube after which the others will fall out. Weld the headstock assembly to the bed, and weld on the left-hand hand rest bracket. Construction of the bracket is straightforward, and no additional details are given, but be sure to use tube with a heavy wall thickness, and weld all round each joint, flashing off the welds flat across the top of the bracket. The welds cannot be strengthened from inside the tubing, so they need to be executed with a good depth of penetration from the outside. The angle grinder will be found invaluable for this preparatory task prior to welding.

THE SPINDLE

Use a length of good quality bright mild steel for this component. Machining this item on a Myford will involve the use of a fixed steady because of the limited size of the spindle bore. Hold one end in the chuck and the other in the steady for initial roughing out. Face and centre drill each end, then drill halfway through from each end until the holes meet. If you do not happen to have an extra long series drill, extend a

standard twist drill by silver soldering a length of rod onto its shank. To do this, turn down a short length of the drill shank to about two thirds of its diameter to fit a hole drilled in the end of the rod. The two are then silver soldered true with each other. In use, withdraw the drill frequently because the swarf cannot escape in the usual way. Still using the steady, machine the 60° angle for the tailstock centre. Drill and ream the No.2 Morse Taper socket, or bore it out, whichever method suits you best. Then machine the 60° angle in the mouth of the socket, thus preserving concentricity. Take a light cut along the outside of the bar for a few inches, just enough to clean up the bar and produce a surface concentric with the Morse Taper socket. Remove the steady, grip the bar on the cleaned up diameter using the four-jaw chuck, centred accurately,

Photo 10.8: Prototype tailstock. (Aluminium casting)

the other end supported on the tailstock centre. Rough down the spindle to a little over 1¼in. diameter as far as the 2in. diameter flange position. Finish turn the 1¼in. diameter observing the close tolerance. Next follow by turning the 1⅛in. diameter, followed by the 1in. diameter. Follow this with the 0.895in. diameter that forms the register for the Myford faceplate.

The next task is to screw cut the two threads, not forgetting that one is left-handed. Do not try using the same screw cutting tool for both as the clearance will be different. Reverse in the chuck before cutting the 1⅛in. x 12 threads per inch thread, check with a dial test indicator as previously, turn the 1¼in. diameter and the 1⅛in. diameter and cut the thread. Mill the two spanner flats using the vertical slide, or file them; alternatively drill a hole for a tommy bar, chamfering both sides.

DUST SEALS
AND RETAINING COVERS

The seals are simply felt washers fitted over the spindle, their outer edges being clamped to the inside end faces of the headstock by the retaining covers. The recess containing the seal needs to be slightly shallower than the thickness of the felt so that the felt is lightly compressed. Wet the felt with oil on assembly and take care that the fixing screws do not foul the bearings by being too long.

SCREW COLLAR AND LOCKNUT

Screw-cut a length which is long enough to make both items, and part them off to keep their end faces square. Drill holes for a 'C' spanner.

MOTOR TABLE SUPPORT

This item is made from ¼in. mild steel plate, 12in. long by 9in. wide. Its exact size is really dictated by the motor to be used. It is therefore wise to obtain a suitable motor beforehand. The mounting holes will naturally have to match the motor's base, and should the motor frame happen to be much larger than that of my machine, then it is conceivable that the plate might require to be slightly larger. Lugs need to be made and welded on to the back of the headstock to support the motor table. Push a length of rod through the holes to

preserve alignment during welding. Matching lugs are welded to the motor table using the rod as before. Weld on the triangular channel supports and give the work completed so far a good clean, after which it may be given a coat of primer followed by a finish coat of paint. Avoid painting the areas where the bearings will fit.

HEADSTOCK SPINDLE ASSEMBLY

Fit the bearings into their housings and bolt on the right hand one. Slide the spindle through, and slide on a dust seal followed by the pulley and drive belt. Next comes the other dust seal and then the other bearing in its housing which should not be bolted on too tightly. The screw collar can be assembled next. A No.2 Morse Taper test bar is now fitted in the spindle taper. This can be made, and is simply a No.2 Morse Taper shank with a plain parallel extension 1in. diameter by 6in. long. Using a dial test indicator on a scribing block standing on the lathe bed, the bearing housings are adjusted until parallel with the bed in both planes. They are then tightened firmly, and two dowels are fitted into each housing to prevent further movement. Tighten the screw collar carefully so that there is

Photo 10.9: Belt drive details

no end play, avoiding the application of excessive pre-loading of the bearings. Tighten the locknut. Application of a little *Loctite* to the threads will prevent them loosening. Grub screws can be provided if preferred. Clamp up the pulley securely.

TAILSTOCK

Machine the barrel first. It is an advantage to have as long a travel as possible consistent with being able to drill the hole down the centre. After the center hole has been drilled, support the Morse Taper end on the fixed steady, and the other end in the four-jaw chuck. Clock up carefully and machine the Morse Taper socket and 60° angle. Remove the steady and support on the tailstock centre. Screw cut the 1in. x 8 threads per inch left-hand thread. Having reversed the barrel, and holding the socket end in the chuck, the other end on the centre, cut the keyway using the vertical slide.

The outer sleeve is turned next. Drill out as much waste as possible before boring; aim for a good sliding fit. Next, clean up the 2⅛in. diameter, so that the steady will hold the work concentrically to bore out the 1½in. diameter recess. If the bar is initially 8in. long to allow for chucking at one end, then the 6in. x 1.5in. diameter can be machined. If the steady gets in the way then make a plug furnished with a centre hole to fit in the 1in. bore, so that the tailstock can be used instead.

Machine to length and face the end. Mill the ⅛in. wide slot using a slitting saw held on a stub arbor in the chuck, the work being supported on the vertical slide. Drill and tap the 4 BA threaded hole, and the 3/16in. BSW hole. The support flanges must be made as a matched pair. Clamp them together and mark out one of them. Measure the actual centre height of the headstock and the offset dimension and use these sizes for marking out. Clamp the flanges on the cross slide and mill or fly-cut the 3 21in. length to clean up and then use the surface as a datum for marking out the ¾in. radius. Much of the waste can be sawn out before machining the radius to size. Next, make the base plate and drill the hole for the clamping bolt. The reinforcing web can then be made. The test bar previously made is used again, this time to align headstock and tailstock. Fit the tapered end into the headstock spindle, and the tailstock outer sleeve is slid on to the 1in. diameter. The base, furnished with the cheek plates, is positioned beneath and the support

flanges and reinforcing web fitted into place. Ideally the support flanges should slide into position without undue force or slackness. The assembly is now tacked together carefully after which it is finally welded securely.

Next, make the hand wheel and handle. Graduate the outer edge if desired; the eight threads per inch thread provides a useful pitch. The key is made initially as a complete disc and then cut into two parts. The 3.7mm hole is best marked out in situ. The assembly can now be painted.

HANDREST SUPPORT

This does not require additional information other than to advise you to resist any temptation to make it from anything other than heavy-gauge material. The cross piece upon which the turning tool will be supported should be not less than ¼in. thick. Because of the angle at which it is welded, any flexing, however slight, will result in the tool taking a deeper bite into the wood, which will cause it to dig in still deeper. Be warned.

STAND

This is optional, as the lathe can be bench mounted if desired. The levelling device is most useful, the majority of floors not being perfectly flat.

The stand is simply welded up from 2in. x 2in. angle iron, and details have been left to the constructor's discretion. Scaling can, however, be carried out from the general arrangement drawing. The shelf is a useful addition, either to hold tools or to carry extra weight. When turning irregular lumps of wood, vibration can be reduced by artificially increasing the weight of the machine by loading of the tool tray with concrete blocks. A book well worth reading which explains this latter point is Peter Child's *The Craftsman Woodturner*.

WIRING

If wiring up the machine yourself take care to ensure that all wiring is well insulated and that protection against chafing of the wiring is provided. It is worth using double insulated conductors for extra security. Run the wiring through conduit so that there is no possibility of damage being caused by the accidental dropping of a sharp tool. A plastic cover must be made to prevent accidental contact with bare wires or the backs of the switches when reaching into the headstock space in order to change speeds. The reverse facility will be found very useful in obtaining a first-class finish on turned work, because that last trace of roughness can best be removed by a touch of glass paper while running the work in reverse. Be very wary of starting the machine in reverse when turning a heavy object mounted on a face plate. The face plate can unscrew itself due to the inertia of the object, and can shoot off across the floor like a Ferrari! Provision of a grub screw to hold the face plate against coming undone is worth considering.

The motor needs to be ½ H.P. or more, and if you do have a choice, then use a motor that has 'soft start' properties to minimize the sudden starting motion. My machine is fitted with a ½ H.P. motor from an old forge compressor, and is powerful enough for me. The lathe was made in 1985, and was built in less than three weeks. Finally, if you do decide to embark upon this project and take pains to construct the machine carefully, you will be rewarded with a tool that will give many years of pleasure.

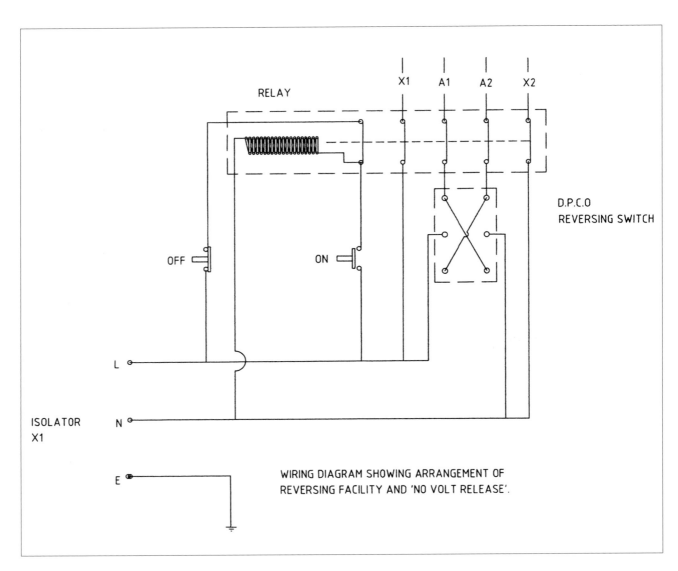

Drawing 10.10: Wiring

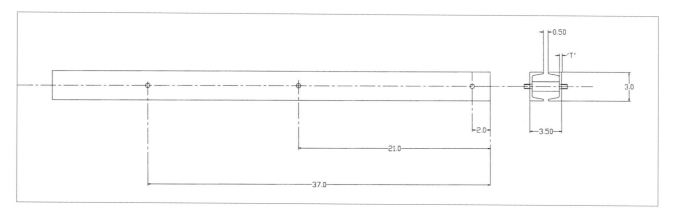

Drawing 10.11: Bed sub assembly

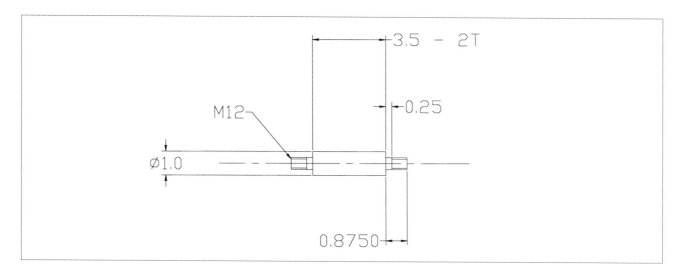

Drawing 10.12: Bed Spacer (3 required)

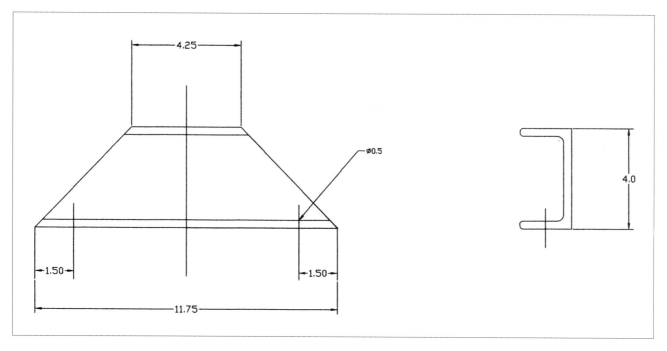

Drawing 10.13: Support flange

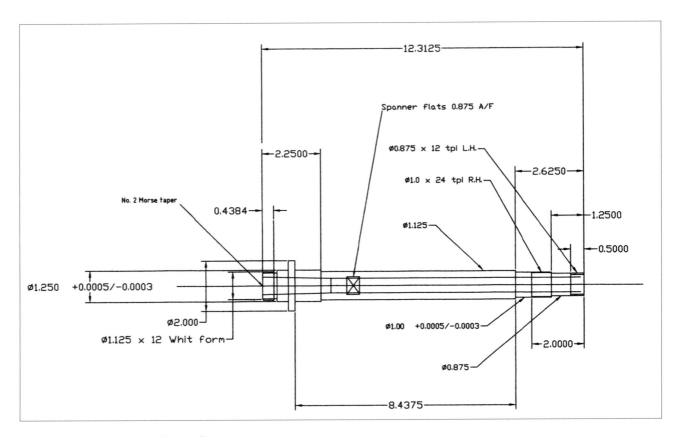

Drawing 10.14: Headstock spindle

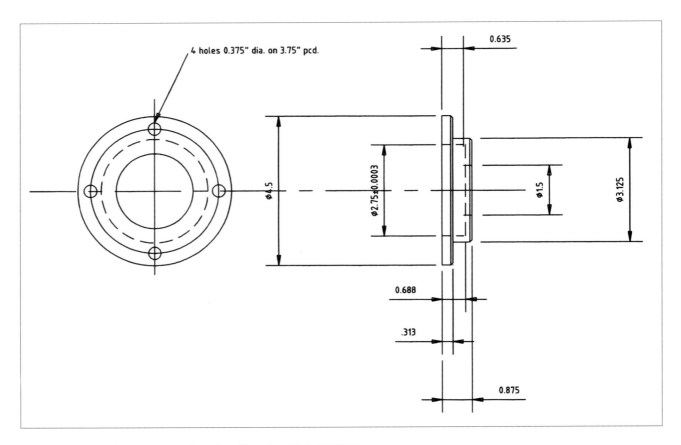

Drawing 10.15: Front bearing housing (Bearing LJ-1.25-2RS)

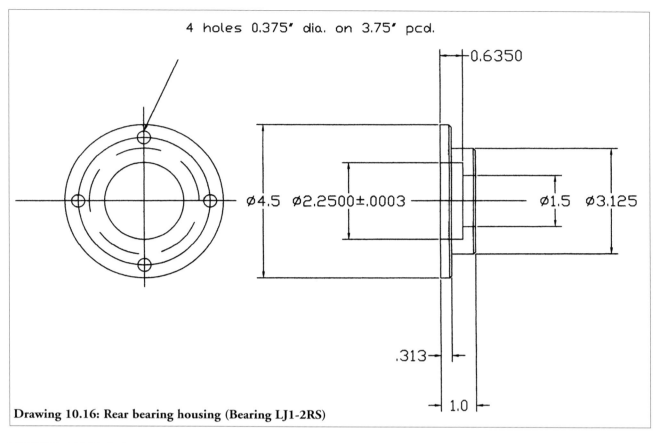

4 holes 0.375″ dia. on 3.75″ pcd.

0.6350

Ø4.5 Ø2.2500±.0003

Ø1.5 Ø3.125

.313

1.0

Drawing 10.16: Rear bearing housing (Bearing LJ1-2RS)

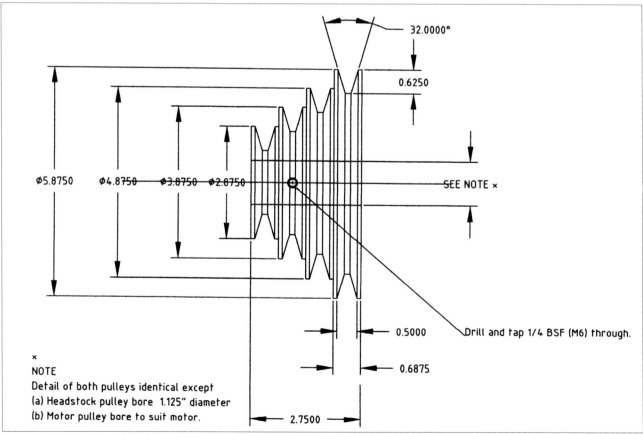

32.0000°

0.6250

Ø5.8750 Ø4.8750 Ø3.8750 Ø2.8750

SEE NOTE ×

Drill and tap 1/4 BSF (M6) through.

0.5000

0.6875

2.7500

×
NOTE
Detail of both pulleys identical except
(a) Headstock pulley bore 1.125″ diameter
(b) Motor pulley bore to suit motor.

Drawing 10.17: Pulleys

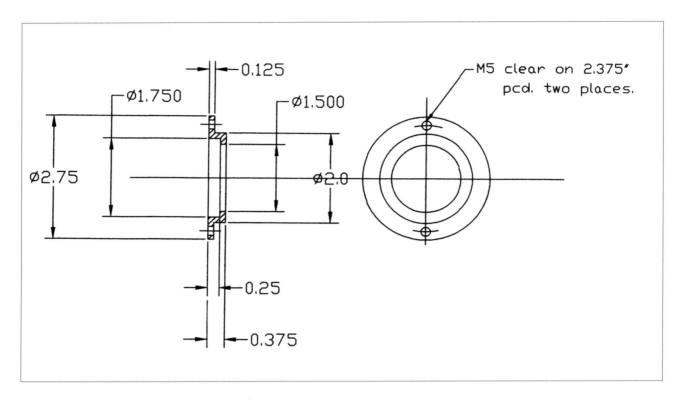

Drawing 10.18: Dust seal housing (2 required)

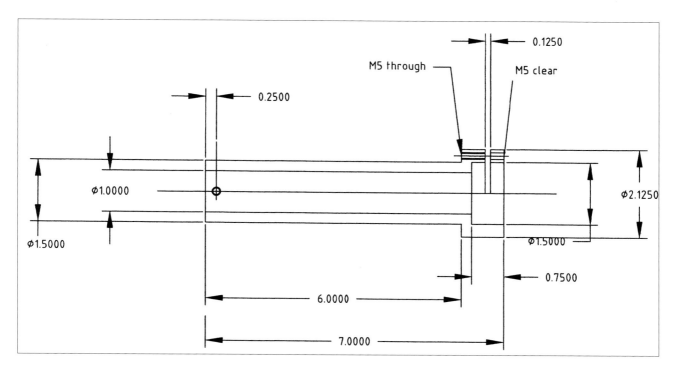

Drawing 10.19: Tailstock outer sleeve

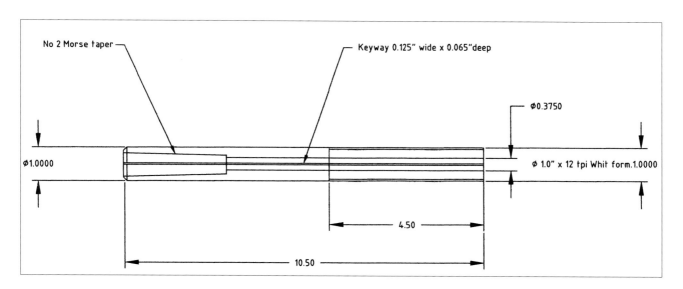

Drawing 10.20: Tailstock spindle

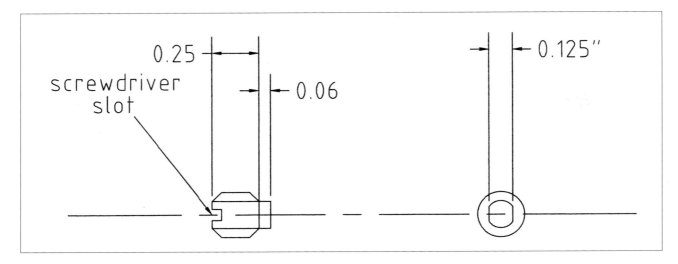

Drawing 10.21: Tailstock spindle key (make from M6 key)

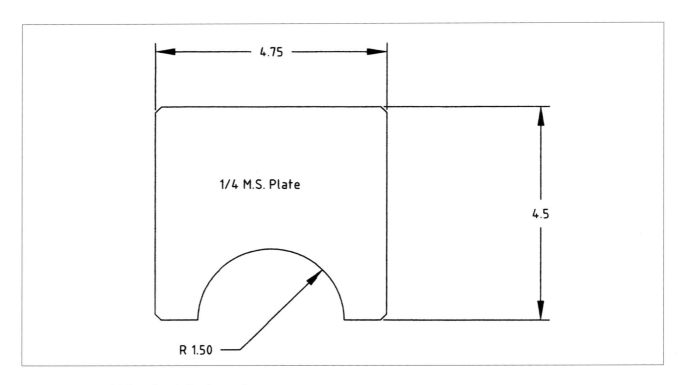

Drawing 10.22: Tailstock reinforcing web

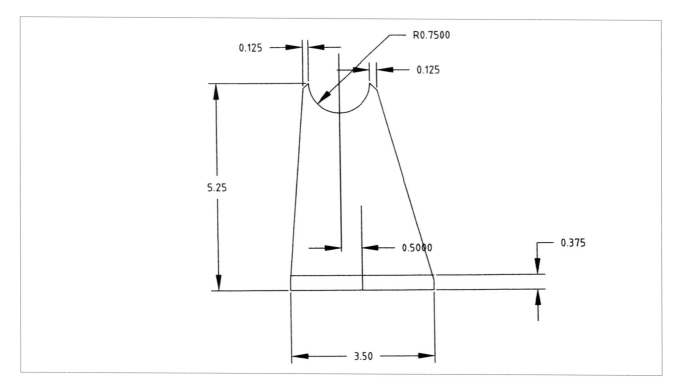

Drawing 10.23: Tailstock endplate (2 required)

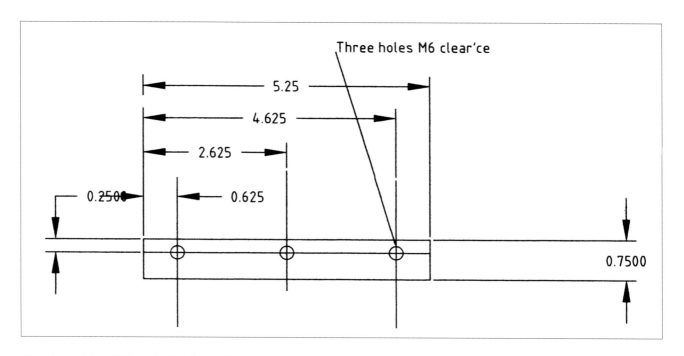

Drawing 10.24: Tailstock sideplates (2 required)

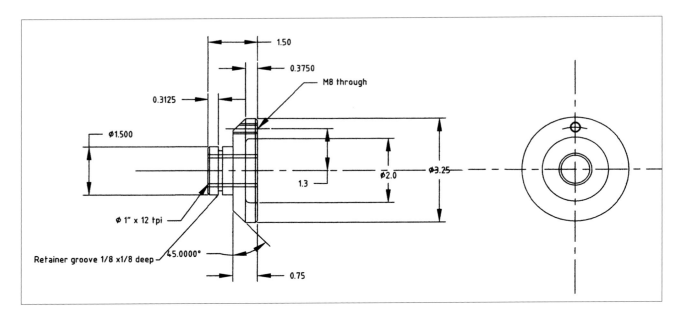

Drawing 10.25: Tailstock hand wheel

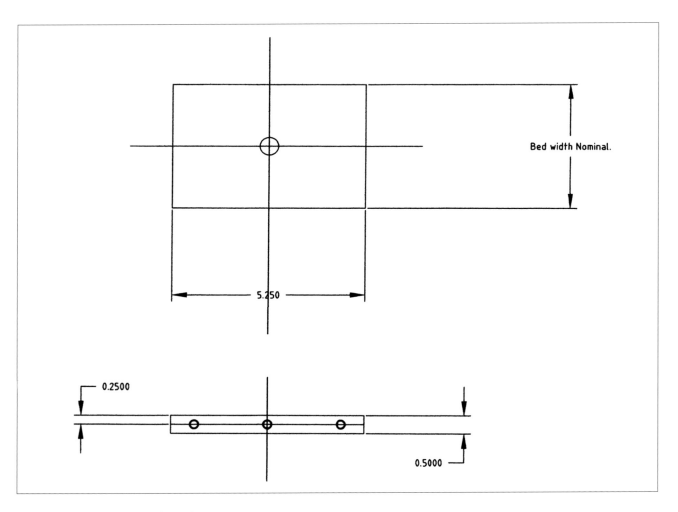

Drawing 10.26: Tailstock baseplate

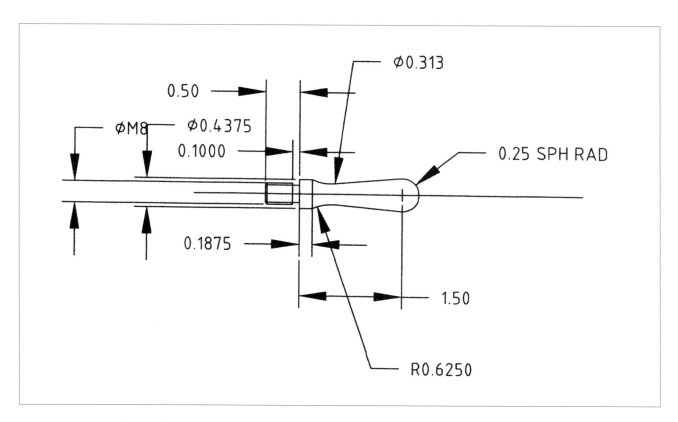

Drawing 10.27: Tailstock handle

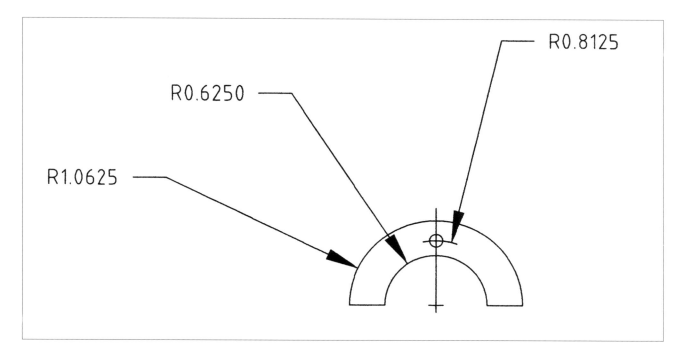

Drawing 10.28: Key (make from 0.125" thich M.S.)

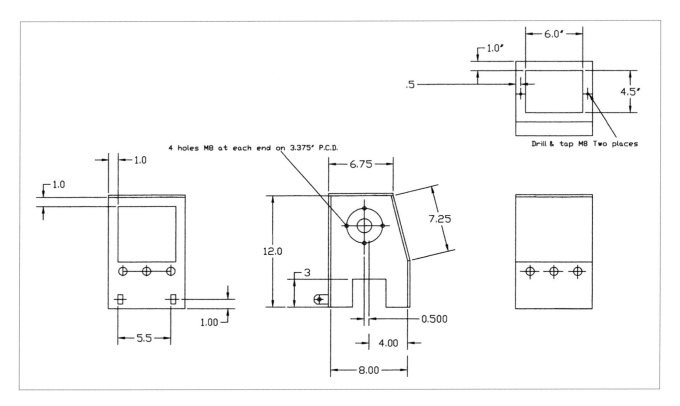

Drawing 10.29: Headstock fabrication

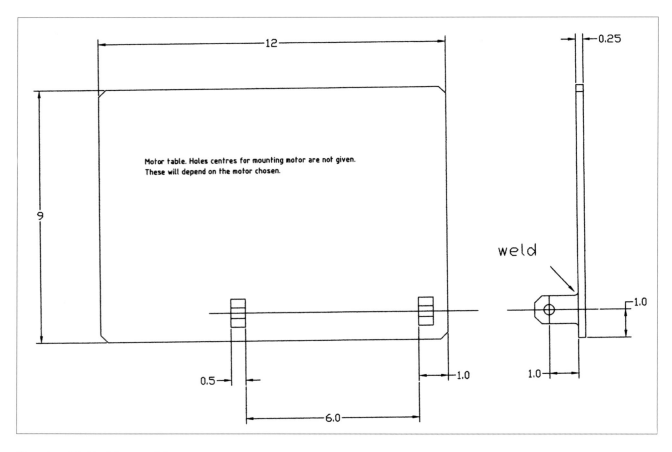

Motor table. Holes centres for mounting motor are not given.
These will depend on the motor chosen.

weld

Drawing 10.30: Motor table

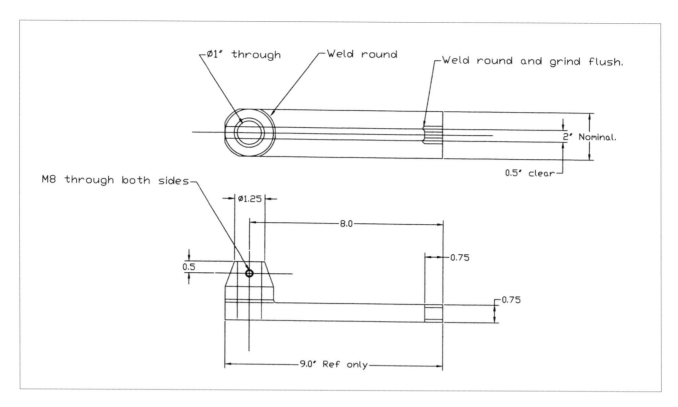

Drawing 10.31: Front rest bracket

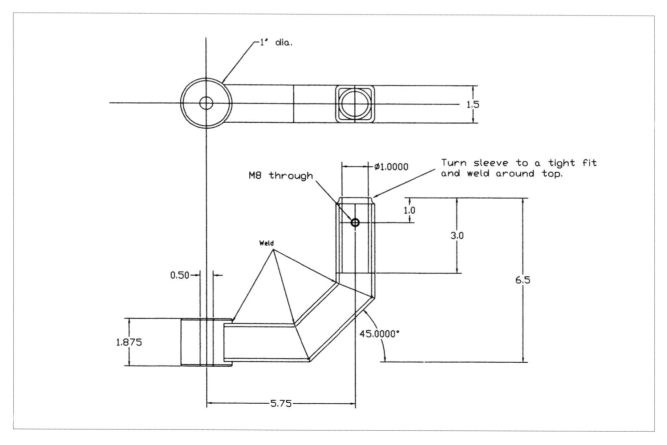

Drawing 10.32: Rear rest bracket

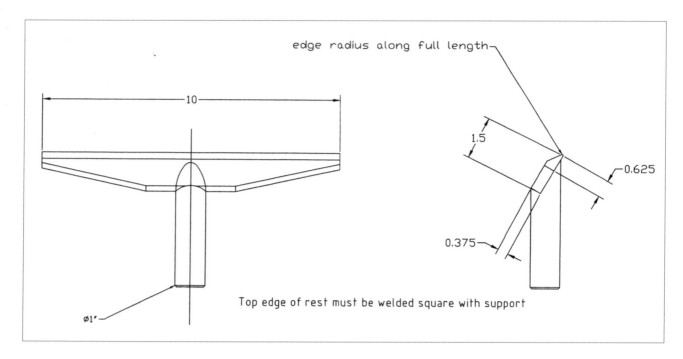

Drawing 10.33: Tool/hand rest

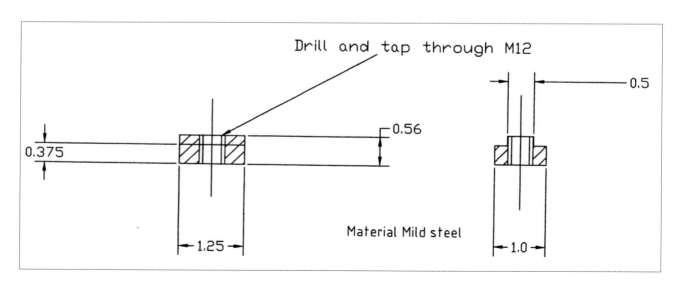

Drawing 10.34: 'T' nut for tool/hand rest fixing

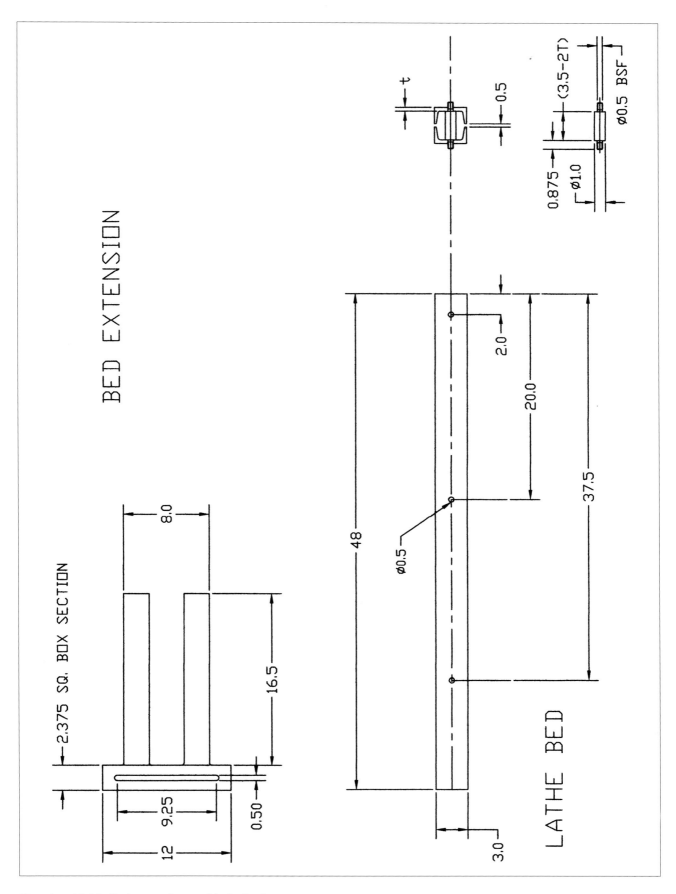

Drawing 10.35: Bed extension and lathe bed

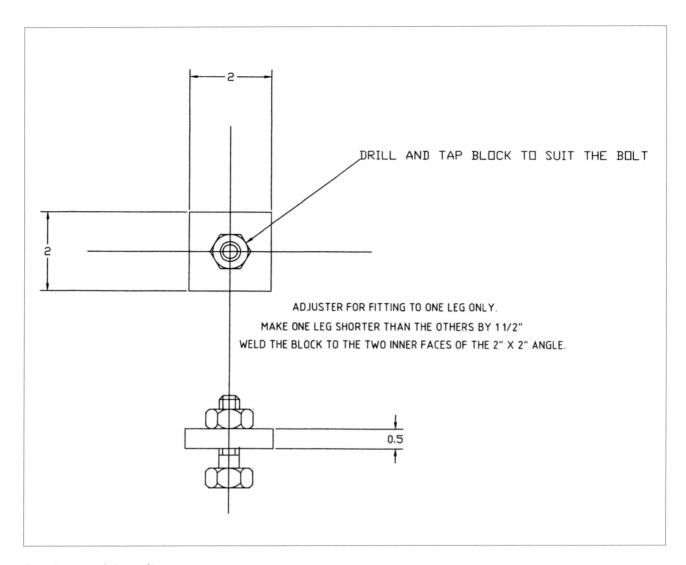

DRILL AND TAP BLOCK TO SUIT THE BOLT

ADJUSTER FOR FITTING TO ONE LEG ONLY.
MAKE ONE LEG SHORTER THAN THE OTHERS BY 1 1/2"
WELD THE BLOCK TO THE TWO INNER FACES OF THE 2" X 2" ANGLE.

Drawing 10.36: Leg adjuster

APPENDICES

POLY-V DRIVE BELTS

The only belt range for which data is given here is the "J" section. This is the most useful for the home constructor or model engineer. The drawing gives the dimensions necessary to enable the turning of pulleys for machine applications. The section of the belt enables the designing of a more compact drive arrangement, as it can be used on pulleys of much smaller diameters than those where the conventional V belts would be used. The "J" section belt can be used where Z, A, B or SPZ section belts would normally be used.

**Photo 11.1:
Poly-V drive belt
("J" section)**

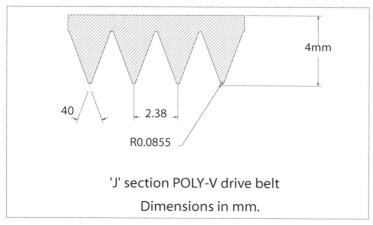

'J' section POLY-V drive belt
Dimensions in mm.

Drawing 11.2: Poly-V drive belt dimensions

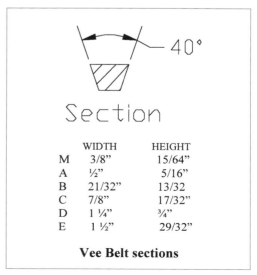

Section

	WIDTH	HEIGHT
M	3/8"	15/64"
A	½"	5/16"
B	21/32"	13/32
C	7/8"	17/32"
D	1 ¼"	¾"
E	1 ½"	29/32"

Vee Belt sections

			EQUIVALENT SIZES FOR DRILLS				
INS	FRACTION	No/Letter	MM	INS	FRACTION	No/Letter	MM
0.0313			0.7938	0.1610		20	4.0894
0.0156	1/64		0.3969	0.1660		19	4.2164
0.0313	1/32		0.7938	0.1695		18	4.3053
0.0400		60	1.0160	0.1719	11/64		4.3656
0.0410		59	1.0414	0.1730		17	4.3942
0.0420		58	1.0668	0.1770		16	4.4958
0.0430		57	1.0922	0.1800		15	4.5720
0.0465		56	1.1811	0.1820		14	4.6228
0.0469	3/64		1.1906	0.1850		13	4.6990
0.0520		55	1.3208	0.1875	3/16		4.7625
0.0550		54	1.3970	0.1890		12	4.8006
0.0595		53	1.5113	0.1910		11	4.8514
0.0625	1/16		1.5875	0.1935		10	4.9149
0.0635		52	1.6129	0.1960		9	4.9784
0.0660		51	1.6764	0.1990		8	5.0546
0.0700		50	1.7780	0.2010		7	5.1054
0.0730		49	1.8542	0.2031	13/64		5.1594
0.0760		48	1.9304	0.2040		6	5.1816
0.0781	5/64		1.9844	0.2055		5	5.2197
0.0785		47	1.9939	0.2090		4	5.3086
0.0810		46	2.0574	0.2130		3	5.4102
0.0820		45	2.0828	0.2188	7/32		5.5563
0.0860		44	2.1844	0.2210		2	5.6134
0.0890		43	2.2606	0.2280		1	5.7912
0.0935		42	2.3749	0.2340		A	5.9436
0.0960		41	2.4384	0.2344	15/64		5.9531
0.0980		40	2.4892	0.2380		B	6.0452
0.0995		39	2.5273	0.2420		C	6.1468
0.0938	3/32		2.3813	0.2460		D	6.2484
0.1015		38	2.5781	0.2500	1/4	E	6.3500
0.1040		37	2.6416	0.2656	17/64		6.7469
0.1065		36	2.7051	0.2570		F	6.5278
0.1094	7/64		2.7781	0.2610		G	6.6294
0.1100		35	2.7940	0.2660		H	6.7564
0.1110		34	2.8194	0.2720		I	6.9088
0.1130		33	2.8702	0.2770		J	7.0358
0.1160		32	2.9464	0.2810		K	7.1374
0.1200		31	3.0480	0.2813	9/32		7.1438
0.1250	1/8		3.1750	0.2900		L	7.3660
0.1285		30	3.2639	0.2950		M	7.4930
0.1360		29	3.4544	0.3020		N	7.6708
0.1405		28	3.5687	0.2969	19/64		7.5406
0.1406	9/64		3.5719	0.3125	5/16		7.9375
0.1440		27	3.6576	0.316		O	8.0264
0.1470		26	3.7338	0.323		P	8.2042
0.1495		25	3.7973	0.3281	21/64		8.3344
0.1520		24	3.8608	0.3320		Q	8.4328
0.1540		23	3.9116	0.3390		R	8.6106
0.1563	5/32		3.9688	0.3438	11/32		8.7313
0.1570		22	3.9878	0.3480		S	8.8392
0.1590		21	4.0386	0.3580		T	9.0932

INS	FRACTION	No/Letter	MM	INS	FRACTION	No/Letter	MM
0.3594	23/64		9.1281	0.6406	41/64		16.2719
0.3680		U	9.3472	0.6563	21/32		16.6688
0.3750	3/8		9.5250	0.6719	43/64		17.0656
0.3770		V	9.5758	0.6875	11/16		17.4625
0.3860		W	9.8044	0.7031	45/64		17.8594
0.3906	25/64		9.9219	0.7188	23/32		18.2563
0.3970		X	10.0838	0.7344	47/64		18.6531
0.4040		Y	10.2616	0.7500	3/4		19.0500
0.4063	13/32		10.3188	0.7656	49/64		19.4469
0.4130		Z	10.4902	0.7813	25/32		19.8438
0.4219	27/64		10.7156	0.7969	51/64		20.2406
0.4375	7/16		11.1125	0.8125	13/16		20.6375
0.4531	29/64		11.5094	0.8281	53/64		21.0344
0.4688	15/32		11.9063	0.8438	27/32		21.4313
0.4844	31/64		12.3031	0.8594	55/64		21.8281
0.5000	1/2		12.7000	0.8750	7/8		22.2250
0.5156	33/64		13.0969	0.8906	57/64		22.6219
0.5313	17/32		13.4938	0.9063	29/32		23.0188
0.5469	35/64		13.8906	0.9219	59/64		23.4156
0.5625	9/16		14.2875	0.9375	15/16		23.8125
0.5781	37/64		14.6844	0.9531	61/64		24.2094
0.5938	19/32		15.0813	0.9688	31/32		24.6063
0.6094	39/64		15.4781	0.9844	63/64		25.0031
0.6250	5/8		15.8750	1.0000			25.4000

BRITISH STANDARD CENTRE DRILLS					
Size	Body dia	Drill dia.	Body dia	Drill dia.	
BS1	1/8"	3/64"	BS5	7/16"	3/16"
BS2	3/16"	1/16"	BS6	5/8"	1/4"
BS3	1/4"	3/32"	BS7	3/4"	5/16"
BS4	5/16"	1/8"			

Tapping Drill Sizes.

METRIC (I.S.O)

Thread	Pitch	Tapping Drill	Thread	Pitch	Tapping Drill
M2.0	0.25	No.51	M11.0	1.50	9.50
M2.0	0.40	No 52	M12.0	1.00	11.00
M2.0	0.45	No.53	M12.0	1.25	10.90
M2.2	0.45	No.51	M12.0	1.50	10.50
M2.5	0.35	No.45	M12.0	1.75	10.25
M2.5	0.45	No.46	M14.0	1.00	13.00
M3.0	0.35	No.37	M14.0	1.25	12.80
M3.0	0.50	No.39	M14.0	1.50	12.50
M3.5	0.35	1/8	M14.0	2.00	15/32
M3.5	0.60	2.90	M16.0	1.00	19/32
M4.0	0.50	3.50	M16.0	1.50	14.40
M4.0	0.70	3.25	M16.0	2.00	14.00
M4.5	0.50	No.22	M18.0	1.00	43/64
M4.5	0.75	No.27	M18.0	1.50	16.50
M5.0	0.50	No.15	M18.0	2.00	16.00
M5.0	0.80	No.20	M18.0	2.50	15.50
M6.0	0.75	No.5	M20.0	1.0	19.00
M6.0	1.00	5.00	M20.0	1.5	18.5
M7.0	0.50	D	M20.0	2.00	18.00
M7.0	0.75	6.00	M20.0	2.50	17.50
M8.0	0.75	7.25	M22.0	1.00	21.00
M8.0	1.00	J	M22.0	1.50	20.50
M8.0	1.25	17/64	M22.0	2.00	20.00
M9.0	0.75	8.20	M22.0	2.5	19.50
M9.0	1.00	7.80	M24.0	1.00	23.00
M9.0	1.25	7.75	M24.0	1.50	22.50
M10.0	0.75	9.25	M24.0	2.00	22.00
M10.0	1.00	23/64	M24.0	3.00	21.00
M10.0	1.50	21/64	M25.0	1.50	23.50
M11.0	1.00	25/64	M25.0	2.00	23.00

British Standard Pipe Parallel

Thread	T.P.I	Tapping Drill
1/8"	28	8.75
1/4"	19	11.8
3/16"	19	19/32
1/2"	14	3/4
3/4"	14	24.50
1"	11	30.75

British Standard Whitworth BSW

Thread	T.P.I	Tapping Drill
1/8"	40	No.39
3/16"	24	No.27
1/4"	20	5.00
5/16"	18	6.50
3/8"	16	O
7/16"	14	U
1/2"	12	10.50
9/16"	12	12.00
5/8"	11	17/32
11/16"	11	19/32
3/4"	10	41/64
7/8"	9	49/64
1"	8	55/64

Brass BSB

Thread	T.P.I	Tapping Drill
1/4"	26	5.3mm
5/16"	26	6.9
3/8"	26	21/64
7/16"	26	25/64
1/2"	26	29/64
9/16"	26	13.00
5/8"	26	14.75
3/4"	26	45/64

British Standard Fine BSF

Thread	T.P.I	Tapping Drill
3/16"	32	No.22
7/32"	28	No.15
1/4"	26	No.4
9/32"	26	6.00
5/16"	22	6.75
3/8"	20	21/64
7/16"	18	9.80
1/2"	16	11.1
9/16"	16	12.6
5/8"	14	35/64
11/16"	14	15.50
3/4"	12	21/32
7/8"	11	25/32
1"	10	57/64

Model Engineer ME

Thread	T.P.I	Tapping Drill
1/8"	40	2.4mm
5/32"	40	3.25
3/16"	40	No.23
7/32"	40	No.13
1/4"	32	No.3
1/4"	40	No.2
9/32"	32	6.1
9/32"	40	6.5
5/16"	32	J
5/16"	40	L
3/8"	32	8.6
3/8"	40	8.9
7/16"	32	13/32
7/16"	40	10.5
1/2"	32	15/32
1/2"	40	12.00

Cycle BSC

Thread	T.P.I	Tapping Drill
3/16"	32	No.22
1/4"	26	No.3
5/16"	26	J
3/8"	26	11/32
7/16"	26	10.25
1/2"	26	15/32
9/16"	20	33/64
9/16"	26	13.5
5/8"	26	19/32
5/8"	20	9/16
3/4"	26	18.25

British Association BA

Thread	Tapping Drill
No.0	5.00
No.1	No.15
No.2	No.22
No.3	3.40
No.4	3.00
No.5	No.37
No.6	2.30
No.7	No.46
No.8	1.70
No.9	No.52
No.10	No.55
No.11	No.56
No.12	1.05
No.13	0.98
No.14	0.75

Unified National Coarse UNC

Thread	T.P.I	Tapping Drill
No.1	64	No.52
No.2	56	1.85
No.3	48	No.45
No.4	40	2.35
No.5	40	No.37
No.6	32	2.75
No.8	32	3.50
No.10	24	No.23
No.12	24	No.15
1/4"	20	5.0
5/16"	18	G
3/8"	16	O
7/16"	14	U
1/2"	13	27/64
9/16"	12	12.20
5/8"	11	17/32
3/4"	10	16.50
7/8"	9	19.50
1"	8	7/8

Unified National Fine UNF

Thread	T.P.I	Tapping Drill
No.0	80	1.25
No.1	72	No.52
No.2	64	1.90
No.3	56	No.45
No.4	48	2.40
No.5	44	No.36
No.6	40	3.00
No.8	36	3.50
No.10	32	No.20
1/4"	28	No.3
5/16"	24	6.90
3/8"	24	8.50
7/16"	20	25/64
1/2"	20	29/64
9/16"	18	13.00
5/8"	18	14.50
3/4"	16	11/16
7/8"	14	20.50
1"	12	59/64

HEAD DIMENSIONS FOR SOCKET SCREWS

			ISO Metric socket cap screws						
Nominal size	M1.4	M1.6	M1.7	M1.8	M2	M2.3	M2.5	M2.6	
Thread pitch	0.3	0.35	0.35	0.35	0.4	0.4	0.45	0.45	
Head diameter	2.6	3	3	3.4	3.8	4	4.5	4.5	
Head depth	1.4	1.6	1.7	1.8	2	2.3	2.5	2.6	
Socket size	1.27	1.5	1.5	1.5	1.5	2	2	2	

			ISO Metric socket cap screws						
Nominal size	M3	M4	M5	M6	M8	M10	M12	M16	M20	M24
Thread pitch	0.5	0.7	0.8	1	1.25	1.5	1.75	2	2.5	3
Head diameter	505	7	8.5	10	13	16	18	24	30	36
Head depth	3	4	5	6	8	10	12	16	20	24
Socket size	2.5	3	4	5	6	8	10	14	17	19
Key engagement	1.3	2	2.7	3.3	4.3	5.5	6.6	8.8	10.7	12.9
Fillet radius.	0.1	0.2	0.2	0.25	0.4	0.4	0.6	0.6	0.8	0.8

			B.A. socket head cap screws						
Nominal size	8BA	7BA	6BA	5BA	4BA	3BA	2BA	1BA	0BA
Threads per inch	59.1	52.9	47.9	43.1	38.5	34.8	31.4	28.2	25.4
Head diameter	0.14	0.161	0.187	0.219	0.219	0.25	0.312	0.312	0.375
Head depth	0.087	0.098	0.11	0.026	0.142	0.161	0.187	0.209	0.236
Socket size	0.0625	0.0625	0.0781	0.0938	0.0938	0.125	0.1563	0.1563	0.1875

			British Standard Whitworth								
Nominal size	1/8	3/16	1/4	5/16	3/8	7/16	1/2	9/16	5/8	3/4	7/8	1
Threads per inch	40	24	20	18	16	14	12	12	11	10	9	8
Head diameter	0.219	0.312	0.375	0.437	0.562	0.625	0.75	0.812	0.875	1	1.125	1.312
Head depth	0.125	0.187	0.25	0.312	0.375	0.437	0.5	0.562	0.625	0.75	0.875	1
Socket size	0.0938	0.1563	0.1875	0.2188	0.3125	0.3125	0.375	0.375	0.5	0.5625	0.5625	0.625

			British Standard Fine								
Nominal size	3/16	1/4	5/16	3/8	7/16	1/2	9/16	5/8	3/4	7/8	1
Threads per inch	32	26	22	20	18	16	16	14	12	11	10
Head diameter	0.312	0.375	0.437	0.562	0.625	0.75	0.812	0.875	1	1.125	1.312
Head depth	0.187	0.25	0.312	0.375	0.437	0.5	0.562	0.625	0.75	0.875	1
Socket size	0.1563	0.1875	0.2188	0.3125	0.3125	0.375	0.375	0.5	0.5625	0.5625	0.625

			UNF & UNC								
Nominal size	No.4	No.5	No.6	No.8	No.10	No.12	1/4	5/16	3/8	7/16	1/2
T.P.I. UNF	48	44	40	36	32	28	28	24	24	20	20
T.P.I UNC	40	40	32	32	24	24	20	18	16	14	13
Head diameter	0.183	0.205	0.226	0.27	0.312	0.343	0.375	0.437	0.562	0.625	0.750
Head depth	0.112	0.125	0.138	0.164	0.19	0.216	0.25	0.312	0.375	0.437	0.500
Socket size	0.0781	0.0938	0.0938	0.125	0.1563	0.1563	0.1875	0.2188	0.3125	0.3125	0.375

WIRE GAUGES

No OF GAUGE	IMPERIAL STANDARD		BIRMINGHAM/STUBBS		BROWN & SHARPE	
	INS	MM	INS	MM	INS	MM
0000	0.4000	10.160	0.4540	11.532	0.46	11.684
000	0.3720	9.449	0.4250	10.795	0.40964	10.405
00	0.3480	8.839	0.3800	9.652	0.3648	9.266
0	0.3240	8.230	0.3400	8.636	0.32486	8.251
1	0.3000	7.620	0.3000	7.620	0.2893	7.348
2	0.2760	7.010	0.2840	7.214	0.25763	6.544
3	0.2520	6.401	0.2590	6.579	0.22942	5.827
4	0.2320	5.893	0.2380	6.045	0.20431	5.189
5	0.2120	5.385	0.2200	5.588	0.18194	4.621
6	0.1920	4.877	0.2030	5.156	0.16202	4.115
7	0.1760	4.470	0.1800	4.572	0.14428	3.665
8	0.1600	4.064	0.1650	4.191	0.12849	3.264
9	0.1440	3.658	0.1480	3.759	0.11443	2.907
10	0.1280	3.251	0.1340	3.404	0.10189	2.588
11	0.1160	2.946	0.1200	3.048	0.090742	2.305
12	0.1040	2.642	0.1090	2.769	0.080808	2.053
13	0.0920	2.337	0.0950	2.413	0.071961	1.828
14	0.0800	2.032	0.0830	2.108	0.064084	1.628
15	0.0720	1.829	0.0720	1.829	0.057068	1.450
16	0.0640	1.626	0.0650	1.651	0.05082	1.291
17	0.0560	1.422	0.0580	1.473	0.045257	1.150
18	0.0480	1.219	0.0490	1.245	0.040303	1.024
19	0.0400	1.016	0.0420	1.067	0.03589	0.912
20	0.0360	0.914	0.0350	0.889	0.031961	0.812
21	0.0320	0.813	0.0320	0.813	0.028462	0.723
22	0.0280	0.711	0.0280	0.711	0.025347	0.644
23	0.0240	0.610	0.0250	0.635	0.022571	0.573
24	0.0220	0.559	0.0220	0.559	0.0201	0.405
25	0.0200	0.508	0.0200	0.508	0.0179	0.361
26	0.0180	0.457	0.0180	0.457	0.01594	0.321
27	0.0164	0.417	0.0160	0.406	0.014195	0.286
28	0.0148	0.376	0.0140	0.356	0.012641	0.255
29	0.0136	0.345	0.0130	0.330	0.011257	0.227
30	0.0124	0.315	0.0120	0.305	0.010025	0.202
31	0.0116	0.295	0.0100	0.254	0.008928	0.227
32	0.0108	0.274	0.0090	0.229	0.00795	0.202
33	0.0100	0.254	0.0080	0.203	0.00708	0.180
34	0.0092	0.234	0.0070	0.178	0.006304	0.160
35	0.0084	0.213	0.0050	0.127	0.005614	0.143
36	0.0076	0.193	0.0040	0.102	0.005	0.127
37	0.0068	0.173			0.004453	0.113
38	0.0060	0.152			0.003965	0.101
39	0.0052	0.132			0.003531	0.090
40	0.0048	0.122			0.003144	0.080
41	0.0044	0.112				
42	0.0040	0.102				
43	0.0036	0.091				
44	0.0032	0.081				
45	0.0028	0.071				

COLOUR OF DIFFERENT TEMPERATURES

			Fahrenheit		Deg. C
Faint red (just visible)			1000		550
Dull red			1300		700
Brilliant red			1450		800
Cherry red			1650		900
Bright cherry red			1850		1000
Orange			2000		1100
Bright orange			2200		1200
White			2350		1300
Bright white			2550		1400
Brilliant white			2750		1500

TEMPERING TEMPERATURES

Temper colour	Deg. C	Tools			
Pale straw	230	Scrapers, turning tools			
Dark straw	240	Drills milling cutters			
Brown	250	Taps,dies, Shear blades.			
Brownish-purple	260	Punches, rivet snaps, reamers,drills.			
Purple	270	Pess tools			
Dark purple	280	Cold chisels			
Blue	300	Springs			
Toughening.	450-600				

TOOL TIP ANGLES FOR COMMON METALS

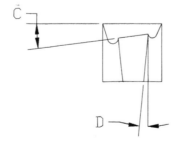
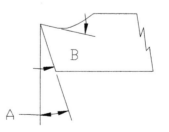

Angle	Cast iron	steel	brass	Gun metal
A	3	3	3	3
B	70	60	80	85
C	15	20	10	5
D	3	3	3	3